Robert Cadell

Sir John Cope and the Rebellion of 1745

Robert Cadell

Sir John Cope and the Rebellion of 1745

ISBN/EAN: 9783337211523

Printed in Europe, USA, Canada, Australia, Japan

Cover: Foto ©ninafisch / pixelio.de

More available books at **www.hansebooks.com**

Sir John Cope and the Rebellion of 1745

BY THE LATE

GENERAL SIR ROBERT CADELL, K.C.B.
ROYAL (MADRAS) ARTILLERY

WILLIAM BLACKWOOD AND SONS
EDINBURGH AND LONDON
MDCCCXCVIII

PREFACE.

In consequence of an article in 'Blackwood's Magazine' of July 1894, entitled "Side-lights on the Battles of Preston and Falkirk," in which a description was given of the battle of Prestonpans and of the part which Sir John Cope played therein, my brother, the late General Sir Robert Cadell, resolved to compile a more detailed and strictly accurate account of the battle and of the circumstances which led to it. This was a task for which he was peculiarly qualified, his home being in the immediate vicinity of the battlefield, and he being familiar from boyhood with the local topography and traditions, and also with the history of the times, to say nothing of his large military experience gained in the Crimea and in India.

The information which he collected could not be compressed into a magazine article, and the work which he had undertaken assumed larger proportions than he had anticipated. Ill-health and absence abroad prevented its completion until within a few days before his death in June 1897. He was thus unable to fulfil his intention of revising his work; and this task, which would have been much better done by him, has devolved on me, with the kind assistance of some friends.

The results speak for themselves. They throw a fresh light on historical events which still possess much interest, and a perusal of the following pages will convince the reader of the conscientious accuracy and patient labour which have been brought to bear on the subject. It will be seen that the sympathy of the author is with Sir John Cope, to whom previous writers, and even popular rhymes, have in his view done injustice. In Scotland the Highlanders engaged in this affair, and their leader, the Prince, the Pretender, or the Chevalier, as he is variously termed, have still a certain amount of popularity, and even recently there have been attempts to revive an interest in the cause in which they were engaged. The reader, whatever may be his sympathies in these matters, will have an opportunity here of acquainting himself with the actual facts; and in so far as they are applicable to Sir John Cope, it is only just that they should be known.

Before concluding these prefatory remarks, it may be of interest to mention the history of the "Sketch of the Battle of Prestonpans, by an Officer who was there." By which of our ancestors the original of this Sketch was obtained is not known, but it has lain in this house for many years. My brother made a copy of it when a boy, before he went to India in 1842, and the original and copy were rolled up together. For some years before his death the roll had been mislaid, and it was sought for in vain. When it was discovered some time after his death, parts of both original and copy were found to have been eaten away by mice; but fortunately, what was destroyed in the one was untouched in the other, and the skilful lithographer has been able to make a complete whole out of the two combined. The several positions taken up by Cope, as shown in the Sketch, correspond exactly with my brother's account of the battle, although he had not seen the Sketch for some years.

T. CADELL.

COCKENZIE HOUSE, *September* 1898.

Postscript.—Since the above was written, a copy of the Plan of the Battle has been found in the possession of the Royal Scottish Geographical Society. The following is the inscription at the foot of the sheet: " Published according to Act of Parliament, Decr. 21st, 1745 "—that is, exactly two months after the battle.

CONTENTS.

CHAPTER I.

PAGE

Object of this work to clear reputation of Sir John Cope—Aspirations of the Stuart family not extinguished by failure of rising of 1715—Prince Charles resolves on expedition against advice of tried adherents—Embarks for Scotland—Encounter with H.M.S. "Lion"—Hesitation of Highland chiefs to join Prince's standard on his arrival—Ambuscade near Spean Bridge—"Raising of the Standard" in Glenfinnan—Divided counsels . . . 1

CHAPTER II.

Unpreparedness of Government to meet the rising—Council of Regency in absence of George II. in Hanover—Persons by whom and mode in which Scottish business was carried on—Troops in Scotland—Sir John Cope (p. 22)—Regency disbelieve news of Pretender's intended rising and disapprove of measures suggested by Cope, and subsequently afraid to act in absence of the King—Help anticipated from Atholl and Breadalbane—Cope's scheme to march into Highlands approved by Regency, and Sir John ordered to attack enemy—Cope's preparations—His staff—Want of artillery—His "fussiness" ridiculed—Contrast with Argyll's action in 1715—Officers left in command in Lowlands (Generals Guest and Preston and Colonel Gardiner)—Royal troops march to Crieff—Cope's interview with Duke of Atholl—Lord George Murray (p. 46)—Not being joined by clans, Cope would not have advanced beyond Crieff, had it not been for Lord Tweeddale's orders 25

CONTENTS.

CHAPTER III.

Cope advances into Highlands—Difficulties of transport—Marches to Inverness rather than attack rebels at Corryarrick—Reasons for this movement—Conflicting counsels in Pretender's camp—He resolves to march on Edinburgh—Repulse of attack on barracks at Ruthven—Causes for clans not joining Cope—Cope's letter to Lord Milton on serious aspect of affairs—Lord Tweeddale underrates their gravity—Lord Lovat's view thereof—Cope marches to Aberdeen and embarks—Pretender marches South—Halts a week at Perth—Replenishes cash-chest and receives reinforcements—Attempted arrest of Duke of Perth at Drummond Castle—Lord George Murray joins Pretender, and practically becomes his Commander-in-Chief 50

CHAPTER IV.

Pretender's march from Perth to Edinburgh—Is not impeded by the Dragoons at the Ford of Frew—Resistance stifled by acts of the authorities—Neglect of King to send troops from Flanders—Career and character of Colonel Gardiner—His shattered constitution—Omission to harass with his dragoons Pretender's army on their march—False sense of security notwithstanding Cope's urgent reports 91

CHAPTER V.

Favourable position of Edinburgh for defence—Refusal of Lord Provost to intrust the trained bands with arms—His opposition to proposals for defence—Professor Maclaurin appointed chief Engineer—4000 volunteers raised—Provost appoints himself their colonel and abstains from appointing field-officers—Prevents sailors being brought from fleet to man guns—Thwarts preparations—Dragoons ordered to Corstorphine—Provost a dead weight on every measure for defence—Dragoons exhausted by excessive duty—Mr Alves arrested for spreading false reports—The "Canter of Coltbrigg"—Dragoons retire to Musselburgh—Then to Prestonpans—And thence, in alarm, to Dunbar . 114

CONTENTS. xi

CHAPTER VI.

Pretender joined by Lord Elcho—Provost's conduct at meeting of Council and at subsequent public meeting—Volunteers give up their arms—Pretender's letter demanding surrender of city—News of Cope's arrival off Dunbar arrives too late—Entry of Highlanders into Edinburgh unopposed—Pretender occupies Holyrood Palace and is proclaimed Regent 146

CHAPTER VII.

Cope disembarks at Dunbar—Colonel Gardiner's opinion of the behaviour of his dragoons—Numerical strength of Royal army—Want of trained gunners—Cope marches to Haddington—A false alarm—Sir Walter Scott's criticism on Cope's not camping at Gladsmuir and awaiting battle there, borrowed from Murray of Broughton—Capture of scouts—Cope marches towards Edinburgh—Gardiner's weakness obliges him to drive in a coach—Cope learns at Seton that Highlanders had crossed Esk and were marching on Preston—Description of field of battle chosen by Cope—Pretender's march from Edinburgh—Learning of Cope's position near Preston—Highlanders ascend to ridge on which Tranent stands—Numerical strength of rebel army—Lord George Murray abandons idea of direct attack, the intervening ground being impassable—The Prince accepts refreshment, and his gallant recompense—Movements of rebel army and Cope's counter-movements—Murray resolves to attack from the east by making a circuit round the marsh—Anderson of Whitburgh volunteers to guide rebel army by path through the marsh—Cope's position during the night 181

CHAPTER VIII.

Calumnies about Cope—He slept on the field—Disposition of picquets, &c.—On report about 3 A.M. that rebel army was moving towards Seton, Cope changes front to the east—Order in which his troops were placed in line—Advance of Highlanders and formation of attack—Only five rounds fired by

Cope's guns—The Dragoons decline to attack advancing Highlanders—Misbehaviour of infantry—Colonel Gardiner mortally wounded—Erroneous accounts of his actions—General retreat—Fowke tries in vain to get cavalry to charge—Wrong word of command given by Colonel Lascelles—Cope's exertions futile—Royal troops seized by panic and make no resistance—Retreat to Berwick—Occurrences after the action—Cope's treasure-chest   212

CHAPTER IX.

The Pretender's behaviour after the action—Colonel Gardiner's death—Paucity of casualties in rebel army—Episodes after the battle—Generous conduct of Lord George Murray to the wounded—His subsequent fate, exile for life—Political effects of the battle—Cope made the scapegoat and held up to ridicule—At his desire a public trial is held—Honourable acquittal—Fowke and Lascelles also exonerated—Cope appointed to a high command in Ireland—Still he is condemned by modern historians, and lastly by Professor Veitch—His death in 1760 253

MAPS.

MAP SHOWING THE BATTLEFIELD OF PRESTONPANS.
[At the beginning.
(From Forrest's Map of Haddingtonshire, 1799.)

PLAN OF THE BATTLE OF PRESTON, 21ST SEPTEMBER 1745.
[In pocket at end.
(By an Officer of the Army who was present.)

LIST OF AUTHORITIES FREQUENTLY CITED.

Henderson's History of the Rebellion, 1745 and 1746.
Lyon in Mourning.
Scots Magazine, 1745.
Chambers's History of the Rebellion.
Culloden Papers.
Lockhart Papers.
Home's History of the Rebellion, 1745.
Jacobite Memoirs of the Rebellion.
Lord Mahon's 'The Forty-five.'
Scott's Tales of a Grandfather.
Ewald's Life of Prince Charles Edward.
Life of Sir John Clerk of Penicuik.
Cope's Trial.
Leaves from the Diary of an Edinburgh Banker.
Burton's History of Scotland.
Gentleman's Magazine, 1745.
Omond's Lord Advocates.
Memoirs of Colonel J. Campbell of Fassiefern.
Wood's Peerage of Scotland.
Caledonian Mercury, September 1745.
Stuart Papers.
Doddridge's Life of Gardiner.
Dr Alexander Carlyle's Autobiography.
Colonel Watton's History of the British Army.
Murray of Broughton's Narrative.
Blaikie's Itinerary of Prince Charles Edward.
Provost Stewart's Trial.
Green's Readings from English History.
Memoirs of the Rebellion. By Chevalier de Johnstone.
Blackwood's Magazine, July 1894.
Introduction to 'Waverley.' Sir Walter Scott.
The Lamp of Lothian.
Dugald Graham's Rhyming History of the Rebellion.
Kay's Compleat History.

SIR JOHN COPE

AND THE

REBELLION OF 1745.

CHAPTER I.

THE sad events of the Rebellion of 1745 will not be forgotten as long as Scottish annals and song endure. The pages of Sir Walter Scott will continue to throw the glamour of romance and chivalry over the deeds and characters of Prince Charles Stuart and his principal adherents; while the verses and music of "Hey! Johnnie Cope!" and other popular ballads will keep in national remembrance the alleged incapacity and ignoble conduct of King George's commander. Contemporary Jacobite writers usually treat this luckless general with some degree of respect; while, amid a crowd of minor accusations, the charges of incapacity, disobedience, treason, and cowardice have for the most part been made by staunch supporters of the Hanoverian dynasty. This latter circumstance has unfortunately been accepted as confirmation of those charges. The leader in the attacks on his reputation was the Rev. Dr Doddridge, whose often incorrect and sometimes impossible statements in his Life of Colonel Gardiner have, without any critical examination, been credited and freely copied by historians from the days of "Ascanius" to those of Scott, Chambers, Mahon, and Ewald. During all this period the real facts, vouched for by soldiers and civilians of the highest standing, have lain recorded, but unread or ignored, in the published 'Proceedings of the Trial of Sir John Cope.' These remarks are particularly applicable to the various accounts of the Prince's first victory at Prestonpans in September 1745, not one of which is free from grave errors both as to occurrences and topography.

It is proposed in this sketch to give a simple narrative of events—all capable of proof—and thereby to show that song-writers, historians, and divines have alike been unjust to a good and gallant officer.

The suppression of the formidable rising in 1715, and the utter failure of the small invasion under the Earl Marischal and the Marquis of Tullibardine in

1719, had by no means extinguished the hopes of the many supporters of the Stuart family. Time and distance seemed rather to strengthen than to lessen the national sympathy for the exiled race; while as yet no germ of loyalty or affection had sprung up to the line of Guelphs. Nearly forty years of experience had not rendered the Union of Scotland with England less disliked by the mass of the Scottish people. The remedies for admitted grievances, which had been suggested by wise and patriotic men like Duncan Forbes of Culloden, and which would have softened bitter feelings between rulers and ruled, had all been rejected. Instead, the Cabinet in London placed their trust in measures calculated to make the whole Scottish nation powerless alike for good and for evil. In the south of Scotland this result had wellnigh been accomplished. The law having now made it actually treason for any subject to call men together for military instruction without the consent of the king, the Lowlanders had become comparatively inefficient as soldiers. In the Highlands, however, the patriarchal system still survived. The supreme command was vested in the chief, whose whole effort was to make his clan efficient as fighting men. A general Disarmament Act had been passed, but its practical effect had been the reverse of what had been intended. It gave offence to all. While the well-affected clans had in reluctant obedience to their chiefs surrendered their arms, the disaffected had not only retained the best part of their own weapons, but had in some cases found means to procure additional supplies.

An important measure, which ought to have told in favour of the Government, had been admirably carried out by General Wade. Great military roads, giving access for regular troops into the very heart of the Highlands, had been constructed, and a chain of fortresses had been established along the line of lakes stretching south-westwards from Inverness to Fort William, and now forming part of the Caledonian Canal. These roads and fortresses would have been of decided advantage in 1745 if the troops for whose use they had been intended had been left in sufficient numbers in the country. But the Continental interests and wars of George II., who, as commander-in-chief, had complete control of the army, had influenced him to denude the country of soldiers.

No warning had been taken from the narrow escape of Scotland from a rising in the previous year, and of England itself from a carefully prepared invasion which was to have been commanded by Marshal Saxe, the best general of France, and accompanied by the Pretender's eldest son, Prince Charles. A great storm alone caused the failure of this expedition at its outset. The Prince, abandoning hope of further immediate aid from France, tried to persuade Keith, the Earl Marischal, a wise and brave Scottish nobleman, who had been exiled for his steadfast loyalty to the Stuart family, to proceed with him to Scotland in order to call out the nation to arms in his cause. But his faithful friend declined to join in an enterprise sure to end in disaster. Charles was much displeased, and the Earl still further raised the resentment of the self-willed young man by baffling his next project, which was to join the French army in a campaign unconnected with the Stuart dynasty. The Prince was then in his twenty-fifth year, and yet he lacked sufficient shrewdness to foresee that a design so unpatriotic as this would have destroyed the personal sympathy which was the first condition of his success in Britain. He was too impatient, however, to endure any longer the humiliations of his trying position. Encouraged merely by Irish officers in the French army, who had nothing to lose in case of failure, Charles reverted to the idea of throwing himself upon the hospitality and loyalty of his adherents in Scotland. And yet these adherents had only recently intimated to him, by his principal agent, John Murray of Broughton, that they could do nothing on his behalf, and would not consider themselves in any way bound to join him, unless he came with a body of 6000 men and 10,000 stand of arms.[1] All the Jacobite leaders in Scotland, with the exception of James Drummond, the titular Duke of Perth,[2] shared in the dismay caused by the prospect of the invidious, and perhaps fatal, dilemma into which they would be forced by an untimely advent. They sent urgent remonstrances to France, which, however, came too late, and they stationed Murray at that part of the Western Highlands where the landing had been threatened, in order personally to warn off the coast their unwelcome guest. Murray remained in the locality during the whole month of June, and then, believing that the project had been abandoned, went back to his house at Broughton. Meantime the Prince hastened the preparations for his expedition, which he announced to his father at Rome in a letter dated from Navarre on the 12th June. In it he falsely stated that he had been

---

[1] Murray, though not older than the Prince, was a gentleman of knowledge and ability, who had, ever since his introduction at the Pretender's Court at Rome in 1741, been his active and devoted partisan. After delivering to Charles the decision of his supporters, he had returned to his estate in Peeblesshire, where he was waiting some change of events more favourable for a national rising, when he was surprised and alarmed by receiving news of the Prince's scheme.

[2] Died at sea, worn out by illness and fatigue, while escaping to France after the battle of Culloden.

invited by "our friends" to go to Scotland, and added, "Let what will happen, the stroke is struck, and I have taken a firm resolution to conquer or to die, and stand by my ground as long as I have a man with me." Brave words, but sadly belied after the battle of Culloden! In another letter of the same date to his father's secretary, he mentions that he had "bought 1500 fusees, 1800 broadswords mounted, a good quantity of powder, ball, flints, dirks, brandy, &c., and some hundred more of fusees and broadswords, of which I cannot at present tell the number. I have also got twenty small field-pieces, two of which a mule may carry; and my casette will be nearly 4000 louis-d'ors : all these things will go in the frigate which carries myself. She has twenty odd guns and is an excellent sailer; and will be escorted by one, and perhaps two men-of-war, of about 70 guns each." Only one, however, of the intended convoy, the Elizabeth, a captured British vessel, now equipped with 68 guns and 700 men, was ready at the time of the sailing. She was now one of the navy of France, whose king had let her out, nominally for privateering purposes, to a Mr Rutledge, an Irish merchant of Dunkirk. By the latter this ship was placed at the disposal of another Irish merchant settled in Nantes, a Mr Walsh, from whom the Prince had hired a privateer, the Doutelle, in which, escorted by the Elizabeth, he actually sailed for Scotland on the 2nd of July 1745.

Charles was accompanied by only seven gentlemen, among whom the Marquis of Tullibardine alone was of high family and influence. He was the eldest surviving son of the first Duke of Atholl, but having been attainted before his father's death for joining in the Rebellion of 1715, the dukedom and estates had passed to his next brother. The scanty dole granted him by the latter during his long exile had not kept him from poverty and imprisonment, and he had welcomed the chance of recovering his birthright.[1] Another attendant was Æneas Macdonald, a banker in Paris, and brother of Macdonald of Kinloch-Moidart. Among the rest were Sir John Macdonald,[2] an officer in the French army, and Francis Strickland, an English Jacobite. The progress of the two vessels must have been tedious, for while still to the southwest of Brest on the afternoon of 9th July they sighted a single British ship boldly bearing down on them.[3] Their foe proved to be the Lion, a man-of-war of 58

---

[1] Henderson's Hist., p. 18.

[2] He saved his life by surrendering as a French officer at Inverness after Culloden (Lyon in Mourning, vol. ii. p. 312).

[3] London Gazette, quoted in 'Scots Magazine,' p. 346, 1745; Lyon in Mourning, vol. i. p. 285.

guns, commanded by Captain (afterwards Sir Percy) Brett, an officer of proved conduct and courage. D'Eau, the captain of the Elizabeth, then came on board the Doutelle and held a council of war, which arranged that the Elizabeth should engage at close quarters, and, if she did not succeed in sinking her opponent with her broadsides, that she should at once run alongside and carry her by boarding; while the Doutelle, being considered to be unsuited from her smaller guns to risk a broadside fight, was to run in and assist when the close combat began. But these arrangements could not be carried out exactly; for the Lion being to windward, her commander contented himself by engaging the Elizabeth within pistol-shot range, and would not allow his ship to be boarded by his more powerful adversary. The combatants continued to hammer at each other till between nine and ten o'clock. By that time the Lion "lay muzzled in the sea," with her rigging cut to pieces and all her masts shot away or heavily injured, and with 45 of her crew killed and 107 (including her captain and all her lieutenants) wounded, many of them mortally; while the Elizabeth had 64, among them her gallant captain and his brother, killed, and 146 seriously, and many more slightly, wounded. Her rigging was not so much damaged as that of the

Lion, but about ten o'clock only one of her lieutenants was left alive and unwounded upon her decks, and he, losing heart, set sail and waited for the Doutelle to come up. As the Elizabeth had not quite carried out the arranged programme, those directing the movements of the Doutelle had drawn off to a safe distance, ready to utilise her swiftness for flight. This prudent manœuvre, as remarked by Æneas Macdonald, "gave those on board the Doutelle time and leisure to observe the management and behaviour of both ships. They fought with equal bravery, but the British sailors showed their superior skill and dexterity, which were highly praised by all on board, as well by the French as by the Scotch; for though the Elizabeth had more men, yet they could not work her so well nor fire so often as the Lion."

Such was the first bloody episode in an enterprise, every episode of which successive historians have disguised with the false lustre of romance. Among these chroniclers Robert Chambers alone possessed the manuscripts of the 'Lyon in Mourning,' the quaint title given by Bishop Forbes to his voluminous collection of documents connected with the Rebellion of 1745. In them were included separate accounts of the action, as told by Æneas Macdonald and Duncan Cameron, his servant, to Dr Burton of York and to the Bishop himself, when they, on account of their participation in the insurrection, were imprisoned with the narrators. Regarding their comparative truth the Bishop wrote that the story of the master " is much more to be depended on " than that of the man, "because Mr Æneas Macdonald is a gentleman who got a liberal education, and was one of the Prince's council, and therefore had an opportunity of knowing things distinctly; whereas Duncan, being only a servant, could know things but imperfectly and at second hand."[1] Yet Chambers, both in his 'Jacobite Memoirs' and in his 'History of the Rebellion,' misled public opinion by extracting what he called "the best parts" of each account, and laboriously dovetailing into one harmonious narrative their conflicting statements. He thus averted the natural indignation which might have been felt if Charles could have been supposed to look callously on while hundreds of brave men were being killed and mutilated for his sake. The same writer, whom even Lord Mahon calls "a warm partisan of the Stuarts," reduces, on the servant's authority alone, to less than one-fifth the actual losses on board the Elizabeth, and otherwise minimises the importance of the sea-fight;[2] while he states that Mr Walsh, from whom the

[1] Lyon in Mourning, vol. i. p. 294.   [2] Chambers's Hist., p. 21.

privateer had been hired, and who had been allowed to come on board for the voyage, "feeling a great responsibility for the Prince's person, declined the proposal of the captain of the Elizabeth that the Doutelle should aid in attacking the Lion"; and he adds, "The Prince several times represented to Mr Walsh what a small assistance would serve to give the Elizabeth the advantage, and importuned him to engage in the action; but Mr Walsh positively refused, and at last desired the Prince not to insist any more, otherwise he would order him down to his cabin."[1] The full statement of Æneas proves these excuses to have been untrue. Even without them no thoughtful person could believe that Charles, who had for months scouted the advice of tried and influential adherents, would have allowed himself, on a matter that nearly affected his personal honour, to be domineered over by a person in the position of Walsh, who had no command in the ship. It would be a mistake, however, to attribute his refraining from joining in the fray to a want of physical courage on the part of the "Young Chevalier," as the Prince was often called. He merely thought it was not worth his royal while to run the risk of the Lion's cannon marring what he believed to be his destiny of re-establishing the divine right

[1] Lyon in Mourning, vol. i. p. 285.

of his family to hold kingly sway over the British realms.

On the Doutelle's coming up to the Elizabeth, another council of war was held, when it was agreed that the crippled Lion should not be further molested, and that the injured Elizabeth should make the best of her way to Brest. The historian Chambers, followed by Mahon and Ewald, for the purpose of adding to the apparent boldness or, as his lordship styles it, "the charm of a romantic enterprise," erroneously states that the French man-of-war carried off the Prince's little store of arms, &c. But these were safe in his own ship. The two Macdonalds and Strickland, who were members of the council, now entreated Charles to put back to Nantes and await a more convenient season; but he only answered, "You will see! you will see!" and ordered the Doutelle's course to be directed towards the Hebrides.

After about a fortnight's voyage the vessel was moored off the little island of Erisca, between Barra and South Uist, whose owner, Macdonald of Clanranald, was head of a branch of that name, and held extensive possessions both among the islands and on the mainland. The old chief, broken down in health, left the management of affairs very much to his brother, the Laird of Boisdale, with whom he was then staying,

and whose property lay in Uist near Erisca. Boisdale
promptly obeyed the summons of the Prince to come
on board the Doutelle. His personal attachment to
the Stuart cause was undoubted, and was afterwards
proved by his forfeiting liberty and risking life and
lands for having given shelter on his estate to Charles,
a hunted fugitive after his flight from Culloden.[1] Yet
he had now the good sense and courage to resist every
argument and appeal made to induce him to call out
the clan. On the Prince's instancing Sir Alexander
Macdonald of Sleat and Macleod of Macleod as neighbouring chieftains who were ready to bring some
2000 or 3000 men to his standard, Boisdale assured
him that these gentlemen were firmly determined
not to join in an enterprise such as the present mad
expedition, which he begged might be abandoned
before it was too late. His advice was unheeded, and
the Doutelle's course was directed towards the mainland, where anchor was dropped next day, the 18th
July, in Loch Nanuagh, a small arm of the sea on the
coast of Clanranald's district in Inverness-shire.

The residence of Macdonald of Kinloch-Moidart
was some eight miles from the anchorage. His brother
Æneas was at once sent to call him on board, and he,
the chief, became one of the first recruits gained by

[1] Boisdale was arrested in 1746, and not released till 4th July 1747.

Charles.[1] He is described as being "an exceedingly cool-headed man, fit for either cabinet or field. He was made a colonel and aide-de-camp to the Prince, and was to have been made a baronet and peer of Scotland."[2]

"Young" Clanranald—for so the eldest son of a chief was called during his father's lifetime—was living in the vicinity. He too was summoned by the Prince, and next day, attended by several of his kinsmen, repaired on board the Doutelle. Two accounts, each given by a Macdonald who was present, but varying in many particulars, describe the ensuing interview. That published by the Rev. John Home in his 'History of the Rebellion' is the most romantic, and is copied by several historians. But Home had been for long a dramatist before he became a historian, and by that time his sympathies had become more Jacobite, though tempered by liberal pensions from a Hanoverian king. The facts are more simply narrated by a Highland officer in the Lockhart Papers. The visitors "were cheerfully welcomed" by Tullibardine, and supplied with a "variety of wines and spirits." It was not till

---

[1] Kinloch-Moidart, when sent by the Prince on a final mission to tempt again into rebellion the island chiefs, Sir A. Macdonald and Macleod of Macleod, was arrested by country-people in Dumfriesshire, and was hanged at Carlisle on 18th October 1746.

[2] Lyon in Mourning, vol. i. p. 289.

after a long conference with the Prince in his cabin that the young chief's resolution to follow the example of his uncle, Boisdale, was so far overcome by the appeals of Charles that he promised to call out his followers, provided that Cameron of Lochiel and other chiefs agreed to join the standard. To further this result, Kinloch-Moidart was at once despatched with letters from the Prince to the chieftains around, including Lochiel and Macdonald of Keppoch; while young Clanranald himself was sent to the island chiefs, the Laird of Macleod and Sir A. Macdonald, whom he found together at the former's castle of Dunvegan in Skye. These potentates, however, influenced by the wise councils of Lord President Forbes, not only firmly refused any assistance in this insurrection, but won him back so far that he gave them "all possible assurance of his own prudence," &c., in the affair.[1] Unfortunately Clanranald on his return to the Doutelle found Lochiel already with the Prince, and learned that his clan had in his absence determined to go out at all hazards, whether he headed them or not.[2] Meantime Charles had sent to Cameron a second letter desiring his immediate presence. The chief thought it his duty to obey, and to explain personally the reasons of his

[1] Culloden Papers, p. 204.   [2] Lockhart Papers, pp. 441-481.

resolve not to join in the enterprise without the stipulated aid of a large body of French troops and previous concert with other leaders. On his way to Loch Nanuagh, Lochiel called on his brother, Cameron of Fassifern, who advised him to impart his determination to the Prince by letter. " I know you," said he, " better than you know yourself. If this Prince sets eyes on you, he will make you do whatever he pleases."[1] Lochiel, however, over-estimated his own firmness. He saw Charles, whose every argument and entreaty he had for some time resisted, conjuring his royal master not to ruin his cause and bring destruction on his faithful friends by pursuing the present hopeless adventure; but he finally yielded to a merciless taunt. " In a few days," said the Prince, "with the few friends that I have, I will erect the royal standard, and proclaim that Charles Stuart is come over to claim the crown of his ancestors, to win it, or to perish in the attempt: Lochiel, whom, my father has often told me, was our firmest friend, may stay at home and learn from the newspapers the fate of his Prince."[2] The chief had, however, some Scottish prudence remaining,

---

[1] Works of John Home, vol. iii. p. 7.
[2] Jacobite Memoirs, p. 22; Mahon's The '45, p. 23; Scott's Tales, vol. ii. p. 239.

for before consenting to call his clan he stipulated that Macdonell of Glengarry should engage, in writing, to join in the rising, and that Charles should give security for the full value of his estate. Lochiel was so much looked up to throughout the Highlands that if he had stood fast to his refusal there can be little doubt the spark of rebellion would have expired.

On the 25th of July the Prince disembarked; and it may be here remarked, that from this same spot on which his feet first rested in Scotland he, after causing a vast amount of bloodshed, ruin, and misery, re-embarked in September 1746, attended by the same Lochiel and Clanranald, who now reluctantly welcomed his landing. Charles was conducted to Clanranald's farmhouse at Borodale, close to the south shore of the loch, whence, after a stay of some days, he proceeded to Kinloch-Moidart's more convenient mansion. Meanwhile the cargo of the ship, which, Æneas Macdonald's journal affirms, "consisted chiefly of brandy, a liquor absolutely necessary in the Highlands,"[1] was discharged, and the Doutelle was sent back to France. Her owner, Mr Walsh, had, besides other services, lent a considerable sum of money to the Prince, who, on his departure, gave him a letter to his father in Rome, begging that there might be conferred on his useful

[1] Lyon in Mourning, vol. i. p. 290.

partisan the dignity of an Irish peerage.[1] The locality of Borodale was admirably suited for an undisturbed organisation of the insurrection. The termination of the military roads from Fort William to Fort Augustus, and thence to Inverness and Stirling, lay within an easy distance, and the garrisons of the forts were so weak as to possess no aggressive power; while the warlike clans inhabiting the mountains and glens bordering upon these routes were all willing, and some of them armed and ready, to rise and fight, provided their chief saw a favourable chance of effecting a permanent restoration of the Stuart family.

All the nearer cheftains—such as Keppoch, Glengarry, and Glencoe — now visited the Prince and received what arms and money were needed to complete the equipment of their men. Murray of Broughton, on receiving the unlooked-for news of his landing, had hastened to join; but not before performing the dangerous duty of getting printed a Jacobite

[1] By the same opportunity he repeated to his father the promise that he would now gain immortal honour by delivering our country or perish sword in hand (Mahon's The '45, p. 25, and Ewald's Life of Prince Charles, p. 77, quoting from State Papers, Tuscany). Neither event occurred; and the latter reckless alternative is somewhat inconsistent with his caution in enrolling himself, before quitting France, as an officer of the Spanish service, and thereby securing to himself, he hoped, the treatment, if captured, of a prisoner of war and exemption from being shot, hanged, or beheaded like an ordinary British rebel.

proclamation, which was at once widely circulated among the supporters of Charles. To these Charles also sent emissaries or letters, reminding them of their promises of aid, holding out prospects of honours and rewards, and calling them to the rising of his standard, which was fixed to take place on the 19th of August in Glenfinnan, a valley surrounded by lofty mountains about twenty miles to the east of Borodale. While thus arranging the rising, " Bonny Prince Charlie" won the hearts of the Highlanders, who crowded to see him, by his handsome looks, his graceful manners, his kindly condescension, and excellence in all manly exercises. Æneas Macdonald records that "in about three weeks, having laid up a large quantity of oatmeal, and a sufficient quantity of brandy" ("two of the most grateful things that could be given to a Highlander"), "the Prince thought it high time to begin to try his fortune."[1] Meantime an incident occurred which gave some heart to the rising clans. So faithfully reticent regarding the preparations for war were even the humblest peasantry, in the neighbourhood of Fort William and Fort Augustus, that, although three weeks had elapsed since the arrival of the Doutelle, the governors of these forts had no reliable information regarding the serious mischief which was brewing. Little danger of attack was there-

---

[1] Lyon in Mourning, vol. i. p. 292

fore apprehended in despatching from the former fortress early on the morning of the 16th of August two newly raised "additional" companies, in all under 100 men. These companies, belonging to the Royal Scots Regiment, had been sent, for lack of more trained soldiers, by Sir John Cope from Perth to reinforce the garrison of Fort William. The intervening distance was about twenty-eight miles, and three-fourths of the long march had been traversed without molestation, when the somewhat fatigued recruits were suddenly assailed in the narrow and wooded ravine near the Spean bridge by a party of Highlanders, placed in ambuscade there by Donald Macdonell of Tiendrish, a kinsman of the Keppoch family. A retreat along the south bank of Loch Lochy to Invergarry Castle was then attempted; but fresh enemies opened fire from the rocks and brushwood on the hillsides, and finally the Glengarry men, led by a son of their chief who had recently accepted a commission from King George in Lord Loudon's regiment, came down in front to attack the little column. Thus sorely beset, after having lost about a dozen men in killed and wounded, including their commander Captain Scott, the troops laid down their arms on "good quarter" being offered to them by Keppoch, who had hastened to the scene with his followers. This promise, however, did not protect them from the humiliation of being three days afterwards displayed at the raising of the standard as living trophies taken in fair war.¹

A great "gathering of the clans" was confidently expected by the Prince to have attended this impressive State ceremony; but for some hours after his arrival at the rendezvous the silent glen was bare of plaided warriors except the bodyguard whom he had brought with himself from Moidart. His relief and joy were great when Lochiel, with 600 or 800 of his Camerons guarding the red-coated prisoners, marched up to the spot. Then the royal standard was unfurled

---

[1] This onslaught is glorified by Chambers and other writers into a "daring exploit," &c. Its hero, Tiendrish, is stated by Bishop Forbes to have been "much given to actes of pious devotion," and to have been the first "to draw blood in the cause." In the following January, while pursuing the king's troops after the battle of Falkirk, he rushed into a party of Barrel's regiment, and mistaking them for French pickets, cried out, "Why don't you pursue the dogs?" Charged with being a rebel, and his white cockade being "so dirty that there was no discovering the colour of it," he declared himself to be one of the Campbell Clan, which by this time had been armed and called out to fight on the side of Government. But General Huske, coming up, called attention to the state of his drawn sword, "which happened to be covered with blood and hair." At his trial at Carlisle he was accused of extraordinary cruelty, which he denied, but admitted seeing "a great slaughter on all hands where he was posted," and he did not claim to have tried, as did Lochiel and the Duke of Perth, to stop the butchery. He is said to have been the original of Scott's Fergus MacIvor in 'Waverley,' and was hanged "on October 18th, the festival of St Luke the Evangelist, 1746," as the Bishop informs us.—(Lyon in Mourning, vol. i. p. 35, and vol. ii. p. 128.)

by the Marquis of Tullibardine, "tottering," we are told by Lord Mahon and other romantic historians, "with old age and infirmities." This is

"The high-minded Murray!—the exiled—the dear!"

of Flora MacIvor's song in 'Waverley.' According to Wood's 'Peerage of Scotland,' the nobleman's age was only fifty-six; and his companion, Æneas Macdonald, describes his ailment to have been gout; while the Laird of Macleod in a contemporary letter to the Lord President remarks, with more candour than romance, that their friend, the Marquis, had "turned an old woman." His need of two supporters was doubtless caused by the fatigue which even a healthy man would have had to endure in displaying on a breezy day a flag "twice the size of an ordinary pair of colours,"[1] during the reading of a long proclamation and a subsequent speech from Charles. Before the close of the day a force of some 1200 clansmen had assembled. The result was disappointing, and the Prince's own commands and appeals having failed, the chieftains on the spot themselves sent letters and messages of remonstrance and reproach to those who had by their absence declined to commit themselves to

[1] Lyon in Mourning, vol. i. pp. 288 and 292; Culloden Papers, p. 208; Lockhart Papers, p. 442.

open rebellion. A serious difference of opinion, moreover, as to future proceedings soon arose. Tullibardine, naturally eager to regain his patrimonial estates, and Murray of Broughton, who had been nominated Secretary of State, and was hopeful of securing the Scottish capital, desired an immediate march to the south; while the chiefs, not liking to leave their homes and districts at the mercy of neighbours on whom they had not full reliance, pressed the necessity of a previous movement to Inverness,[1] which, they thought, would force the powerful clans of Grants, Frasers, Mackenzies, Macintoshes, and others who still held aloof, to declare their fealty to the Prince Regent, as Charles now styled himself. This measure, they urged, would give stability to the enterprise, and enable them to march south with a strength which would give confidence to their friends in the Lowlands. Charles decided to adopt the plan of the advisers whom he had known abroad. In this he was probably supported by the Irish officers who had joined him.

[1] Lockhart Papers, p. 442.

CHAPTER II.

The time chanced upon for Prince Charles's venture, and the locality chosen, were favourable to a first success. There was no force ready to face the danger. George II. had in the previous May betaken himself to his beloved Hanover, and was engrossed with Continental intrigues and wars. A Council of Regency had been nominated to conduct in his absence the domestic affairs of Britain, but its power was much lessened by the personal rivalry of the members, and by their general dread of taking any important step without the expressed sanction of a wilful king. Among the Lord Justices—for so the Regency was called—were three statesmen specially versed in Scottish affairs,—the Earl of Stair, who commanded the troops in South Britain, as England was then officially called; the Duke of Argyll, then the most powerful nobleman in Scotland; and the Marquis of Tweeddale. The last held the office of Secretary of State for Scotland, which had been revived in his favour in 1742, and which, after his dismissal in January 1746, was allowed to lie dormant for upwards of a century. His appointment had given offence to the Argyll family, whose ducal chief, while he bore the title of Lord Ilay, had managed the affairs of the northern kingdom during the long administration of Sir Robert Walpole, and who at the period of the outbreak was staying at his Roseneath mansion in Dumbartonshire. The two noblemen and their parties had not been able to agree as to who should be named as lord-lieutenants. This dispute was one of the reasons why no one had been for some years gazetted to these offices, in which alone was vested the military organisation of counties in case of sudden emergency.[1] The Scottish Secretary in London transacted business through a sort of local State Council which usually met in Edinburgh, and was composed of the principal dignitaries of the Court of Session. At its head was the Lord President, Duncan Forbes of Culloden, than whom no man in Scotland was better acquainted with national feelings, and more respected and trusted, alike for his kindliness and his wisdom, by all political parties. His associates in Council were Andrew Fletcher, Lord Milton, who was Lord Justice-Clerk, and had long acted under Lord

---

[1] Life of Sir J. Clerk, p. 181; Culloden Papers, p. 205.

Ilay as sub-Minister for Scotland; Robert Craigie of Glendoich, the Lord Advocate; and William Grant of Prestongrange, the Solicitor-General. All these gentlemen had—from family connection and otherwise—intimate knowledge of the affairs of Scotland and its leading men. It was Sir John Cope's duty to consult with these "servants of the Crown," as they were styled, and to be influenced by their advice when it harmonised with his military orders and his own opinion as a practical soldier.

The troops in Scotland at this time numbered less than 3000 men, and many of the officers were absent. The cavalry consisted of Gardiner's and Hamilton's dragoons. Chambers and other historians have erroneously styled them "newly raised" regiments; they had, in fact, been raised in 1715, and were therefore for the most part "old soldiers," although they had never seen any active service. They were broken up into small detachments scattered among the various Lowland towns, near which, according to the custom of the period, their horses were out at grass. The infantry consisted of three and a half regiments, only one of which, Guise's, was an old corps, and it was dispersed throughout the forts and barracks in the North. The rest were the youngest battalions in the army, having been raised in 1741. There were also six very weak "additional" companies of recruits, enlisted to make good the casualties in the Scotch regiments serving in Flanders, and some companies of Lord John Murray's and Lord Loudon's Highlanders, on whose fidelity no reliance could be placed.

The commander-in-chief of the royal forces in North Britain at this time was Sir John Cope,[1] that appointment having been conferred on him in February 1745. Unfortunately his nomination incensed many influential people in the North, who thought that friends of their own had higher claims than the English general. This feeling and the political condition of Scotland tended to prevent a friendly, or even an impartial, judgment being formed regarding his military conduct.

During the first months of 1745 the Government had been informed that rumours of probable disturbance prevailed throughout the Highlands, and, after the disastrous battle of Fontenoy in April, a rising had been dreaded. No intimation, however, of actual danger was given at Edinburgh till, early on the

[1] Cope was sprung from an old and knightly family which owned extensive estates in the south of England, and he entered the army in 1707. During his military career he gained considerable experience in the field, and won the red ribbon of the Bath while fighting at Dettingen under the eye of George II.—no bad judge of soldierly prowess. He was member for Orford, in the county of Suffolk, in the Parliament which met on 4th December 1741; and he married Jane, youngest daughter of Anthony Duncombe and sister of the first Lord Feversham.

morning of the 2nd of July, Lord President Forbes called on Sir John Cope and acquainted him with a report then current that the Pretender's eldest son was about to land for the purpose of heading a rebellion in person.[1]

While Lord President Forbes did not give complete credence to the story, he thought it quite possible that a small expedition bent on some desperate enterprise for the purpose of creating alarm might have been despatched by the Court of France. In transmitting the intelligence to Lord Tweeddale, Cope earnestly requested that a supply of arms might be promptly sent from the Ordnance in London for issue, in case of need, to the well-affected but unarmed clans and other well-known friends, whose present helpless condition he depicted. The Regency refused to give any immediate order, and it was not till August that Cope was informed that the inadequate number of 5000 stand of arms would ere long be placed at his disposal. Apprehensions becoming more grave, a council of "the king's servants," attended by Sir John, was held on the 9th of July to consider what precautionary steps should be taken. When reporting the meeting to Tweeddale, the General stated that he had ordered the dragoons to be ready to take

[1] Cope's Trial, p. 205.

up their horses from grass and to collect at short warning; that he had called in as many out-parties as possible; and that he had desired General Preston "to repair forthwith to his command of Edinburgh Castle, which place" he pointed out "to be of the greatest importance of any in Scotland." He also begged that none of his small force might be taken away from him, and that all absent officers might be ordered by the Regency to return at once to their posts. These orders and suggestions met with prompt disapproval. He was told that he was needlessly alarming the country. Thus nearly a month of precious time for preparation was lost before Government was itself alarmed by hearing from France that King Louis was meditating an invasion, and that Prince Charles had actually sailed.[1] Tweeddale credited the first piece of news, which was incorrect, but disbelieved the last, which was true; and he conveyed to Cope the "pleasure" of the Lords Justices that he should now carry out the measures with regard to the cavalry.[2] A few days before, the Marquis had written to Sir John telling him that the Regency would not comply with his request for the recall of absent officers, in fear of its too much alarming his Majesty's subjects, but "earnestly re-

[1] Cope's Trial, p. 110.   [2] Ibid., p. 109.

commending" him to "give orders, as of his own authority and in a private manner, to such officers to repair immediately to their regiments." Those whose leave was thus cut short, and their friends, naturally thought that "the fussy General," as he was called, who was thus inconveniencing them, was acting out of a feeling of personal apprehension not entertained by Government; and many did not comply with the private mandate till, after two further appeals from Cope, the command was repeated in the 'London Gazette' of the 12th August.

In July Sir John made a rapid ride to Aberdeen, where he reviewed Guise's regiment prior to despatching it, with happy forethought, to reinforce the weak garrisons of Fort George, Fort Augustus, and Fort William. On the very day of his receiving the news of the Prince's embarkation, he reported to Tweeddale an energetic commencement of the sanctioned concentration of troops, and again brought to notice their scanty numbers. He at the same time pressed for more arms; for artillerymen, of whom there was a total want; and, above all, for money, which he described as being "a necessary spring to cause the friends of Government to act with spirit."

The Regency was now slowly awakening to a sense of general danger; but in the absence of the king, whose return they had already urged, they did not dare to act with the needed energy. Among other measures, they desired to secure the services of the numerous but disarmed Campbell clan, and thought they might attain that object by authorising Tweeddale to "hint" to Cope that a supply of arms might ere long be placed at his disposal, and that, in case the Duke of Argyll desired it, he, Sir John, was at liberty to hand them over.[1] This, however, was "to be kept a secret, to prevent applications of a like nature from others, to whom, perhaps, it may not be proper to distribute arms." Cope was aware, of course, that the Duke could call out a force of more than double the number of all the royal troops in Scotland, and he at once wrote, proffering the weapons and begging his Grace's advice and aid. Cope received no written reply, but on the 16th August Argyll passed through Edinburgh on his way to London and conferred with him. The Duke declined to accept the arms thus secretly tendered to him, and declared that, "till Government made it lawful for him to do such service as might be in his power, he durst not even defend himself."[2] His Grace doubtless alluded to that law which made it treason

---

[1] Letter from Tweeddale to Cope, 1st August 1745, 'Cope's Trial,' p. 111.
[2] Cope's Trial, pp. 174, 14.

for any subject to gather men in arms without the king's authority, and which, even at the present juncture, neither the Regency nor his Majesty thought fit to relax.

It was not till the 8th of August that the news of the actual arrival of Prince Charles reached Edinburgh. The information was contained in a letter to Cope from Fletcher, the Lord Justice-Clerk, who was staying at Roseneath with the Duke of Argyll. Next morning Forbes, the Lord President, called "in his boots" with confirmatory intelligence, and after consulting with the General rode at once towards his home at Culloden, whence he could best exercise his great influence over the Highland chiefs. In reporting the facts to Tweeddale, Cope again asked for men, officers, arms, and money. In a second letter [1] he explains that the measure which "the king's servants" had agreed with him as the best to meet the emergency, was that all the available infantry should forthwith assemble at Stirling, and that as soon as provisions were available the force should march under his own command by the military road to the chain of fortresses from Inverness to Fort William, for the purpose of "trying to check the proceedings of his Majesty's enemies." This proposal, however, was

[1] Cope's Trial, pp. 114, 117.

conditional on his "hearing nothing to alter the design." The Lord President was strongly "of opinion that from the number of well-affected clans, the intended rebellion could not rise to a great head, but that it could be crushed in the bud."[1] He was confident, too, of being able to raise a large body from the friends of Government in his own neighbourhood. For the equipment of these hoped-for allies 1000 stand of arms were despatched from Leith to Inverness in the Happy Janet, one of the king's sloops of war, which were under the command of the Lord Provost of Edinburgh, Mr Stewart, in his capacity of "Admiral of the Forth." A difficulty as to utilising this vessel's services, which was only overcome by an Admiralty order,[2] was the overt obstruction on the part of this functionary, who was the cause of much of Cope's later want of success, and who, according even to Chambers, "acted throughout exactly as might have been expected of a Jacobite who wished to keep a fair face towards the Government."[3] The idea of the proposed movement was that, even in the event, which was considered improbable, of the available force with the addition of expected Highland allies proving to be unable to disperse the rebel

---

[1] Cope's Trial, p. 5 *et seq.*   [2] Ibid., pp. 14 and 120.
[3] Chambers's Hist., p. 98.

gathering, it would at least secure the northern forts, and, interposing a barrier between the enemy and the wavering or friendly clans, form a centre round which the latter might collect in formidable numbers. The perplexing dilemma in which these latter clans now found themselves is graphically described in letters, written on the very day of the raising of the standard, to the Lord President at Culloden and to Cope at Edinburgh by Macpherson of Cluny, whose district lay in Lochaber.[1] He states that, "contrary to his lordship's expectation, the generality of Highlanders on his west were in arms," and that, when they began their projected march south, he and his clan must either join them or be burnt out. He points out that starving, burning, and killing may probably determine not only his own people but those of Speyside and far beyond to join the Prince. He deprecates an encampment of the General's troops at Stirling, and urges an immediate march northwards. The chief's forebodings as to ravaging proved too true, but it was the Duke of Cumberland's soldiers who, after the battle of Culloden, pillaged his country and burned his home.

Cope had fully realised, and had pointed out to the "king's servants," that, in a march through the moun-

[1] Culloden Papers, p. 373.

tains and ravines on his proposed route, it was of the last importance that his force should be joined by bodies of Highlanders from the adjacent districts. Letters were accordingly despatched by the General to several chiefs of whose loyalty he was assured, claiming their support and offering arms and payment to their followers. Among these were the Duke of Atholl, through whose extensive territories the road for the most part ran, and Lord Glenorchy, who at Taymouth was managing the affairs of his aged father, the Earl of Breadalbane. These noblemen in their replies [1] dwelt strongly on their zeal for the king's service, and stood on no punctilio like the Duke of Argyll as to obtaining the royal sanction before calling out their vassals. Atholl, moreover, wrote to Cope that he would "endeavour, not only to keep" his people "in their duty to the king, but even to make them serviceable as far as shall be required of them. In consequence," he adds, "of what my Lord Advocate and the Solicitor wrote me, I have appointed Lord George Murray," his brother, "a sheriff deputy for this country, to give the necessary directions for furnishing his Majesty's troops with everything required that the country can provide, if they are to march northward by Crieff and Taybridge."

[1] Cope's Trial, dated 13th and 14th August 1745, p. 132.

This letter was written after the Duke had entertained at his castle of Blair the Lord President on his ride to Culloden. The latter wrote to Cope, saying that his Grace was "raising all his tenants that he could depend upon," and expressing his "hopes that other well-affected lords would do the like." [1]

Lord Glenorchy on his part wrote to Cope, "I can answer for a considerable body of men for the service of Government, if I had arms and ammunition for them; but I don't know how far self-preservation may operate on men, threatened by others with destruction, if they don't join them." [2] Again, six days after, he wrote, hoping to meet Cope at Stirling, and adding, "I don't pretend that I could absolutely stop them if I had arms, but I believe I could harass them, and at least retard their march." [3] The distance from Stirling to Fort Augustus was only 105 miles; and as either the Breadalbane or the Atholl clansmen were far more numerous than the whole rebel gathering, and as Cope intended to carry arms with him for the equipment of all willing men, he had ample reason to anticipate easy and safe progress as far as Garvamore, which was within one long march of the fort. Garvamore was on the precincts of the district over which Cluny reigned as head of the Macpherson

[1] Cope's Trial, p. 14.   [2] Ibid., p. 134.   [3] Ibid., p. 179.

clan, and that chief was not only urging Cope's advance, but was at the time recruiting in Lochaber regular soldiers to complete his company in Lord Loudon's new Highland regiment.

The Regency fully approved of Sir John's scheme, and repeatedly added to it their own commands to attack the rebels wherever they were to be found.[1] On their receipt of an incorrect but not improbable report, dated Fort William, 7th August, that 2000 French troops had landed near that place, the General was desired not to diverge from the positive orders to attack, already conveyed to him in successive despatches, even if the disembarkation of this large force proved to be a fact. Sir John had pointed out to Government the danger of leaving the Lowlands so much denuded of troops, stating "the absolute necessity of a reinforcement," and had suggested that, as a small help, five companies of Lee's regiment might be moved from Berwick for the safety of Edinburgh; and he had also alluded to the possibility of circumstances arising which would make the exact execution of his plan "improper for the king's service." The suggestion was ignored; but Lord Tweeddale informed him that "orders are sent to North British Fusileers to go to Leith" from Ostend, "which will be some additional strength to you"; and he shortly afterwards

[1] Cope's Trial, pp. 120, 123, 128-130.

added that the orders of Government "as to the crushing in the bud any insurrection were not to be neglected from any consideration of what might afterwards happen in other and more distant parts."

Sir John, on hearing of the Prince's landing, had not lost an hour in buying up all the biscuit in Edinburgh and Leith, in anticipation of the sanction of Government to his plans, and through the Lord Advocate and local authorities had arranged that "all the ovens in Leith, Stirling, and Perth were to be kept at work day and night, Sunday not excepted, to provide biscuit, which in no other way was to be got. There was none to be got in the country the army was to march through." The three weeks' supply required was not ready for ten days; but the slowness in the baking did not practically delay the march. Money was as necessary as food, and the sum demanded by Cope on the 3rd August was not in his hands till the 19th. The specie was at once packed on his own coach-horses, which had been held in readiness for the purpose, and despatched under an officer's guard of cavalry, while within an hour of its receipt the General himself was on the saddle to join his men at Stirling.[1] Meantime he had selected a good working staff. His adjutant-general was Colonel

---

[1] MSS. in the Writers to the Signet Library. Evidence of Major Mossman and Mr Jones in Cope's Trial.

the Earl of Loudon, an excellent officer in the prime of life. His quartermaster-general was Major Caulfield, who had served under General Wade and other commanders-in-chief in surveying and constructing the Highland roads. Mr Griffith, who had been for forty years master-gunner of Edinburgh, had charge of the ordnance and commissariat train. Colonel Whiteford, an Ayrshire gentleman, was employed on general staff duties, and had special charge of the artillery. He was the original of Sir Walter Scott's "Colonel Talbot" in 'Waverley.'

Brave though the Highlanders were, they still cherished an almost superstitious dread of artillery and cavalry. Cope, therefore, to make "a show" of cannon,[1] took with him four very light $1\frac{1}{2}$-pounder galloper guns and four small mortars, the latter being a kind of ordnance only useful for shelling an enemy out of a fixed position. He had little confidence in their power of slaughter—the less so as his request for trained soldiers had not been complied with, and his only artilleryman was "one old man who was a gunner that had belonged to the old Scots Train"[2] before the union of the kingdoms in 1707. Three invalid veterans of old Scots infantry regiments were told off to assist in artillery duties. Good forage for

[1] Cope's Trial, p. 118.   [2] Colonel Whiteford, Cope's Trial, p. 54.

horses being unprocurable, and cavalry being of little practical use among mountains, Sir John decided to leave behind him the two regiments of dragoons, for the purpose of guarding the district between Edinburgh and Stirling, a country over which such a force could, if commanded with ordinary intelligence and courage, work with telling effect against even a numerically larger force of irregular foot soldiers.

A considerable number of the higher classes in Edinburgh and its vicinity were at this time Jacobites, and the majority of those who were callous or even adverse to the Stuart cause, resented at heart the humiliating condition of helplessness to which their country had been reduced by the royal and ministerial authorities in England. The feelings of both of these sets, who together formed the bulk of the educated society of the capital, found some comfort in now throwing ridicule on the English general, whose motives of action were either unknown or misrepresented. "His commendable zeal and diligence"—to use the words of Colonel Whiteford—"by the art of the disaffected, became the subject of most people's mirth."[1] His letters are modest and straightforward, and show a truer apprehension of the situation than any other prominent actor of the period, whether

[1] Cope's Trial, p. 50.

soldier or civilian. Yet some of his contemporaries denounced his supposed indifference to all warnings of danger, and charged him with disobedience in not promptly carrying out the wise orders of Government for an immediate advance;[1] while others jeered at his "fussiness" in pushing on the necessary preparations, and at his having already "in his imagination devoured all the rebels" before even beginning the march. Sir John's plan of campaign has also been unfavourably contrasted with the strategy of the Duke of Argyll, who, when commanding the royal troops in 1715, had waited for months at Stirling till his opponent, the Earl of Mar, advanced against him from Perth. The difference in most of the circumstances of the two rebellions were forgotten. In 1715 the Disarmament Act had not been passed. Friendly or wavering clans were fully armed, and consequently could not with impunity be harried or forced against their wills to take a side in the dynastic contest. And at the outbreak of the former rising almost all the chiefs in the then roadless districts between the southern margin of the Highlands and Inverness had joined the Jacobite cause. It was now Cope's clear duty promptly to protect, if he could, the well-affected or neutral Highlanders from being bullied into be-

---

[1] Henderson's Hist., p. 32; Sir J. Clerk's Autobiography.

coming rebels, and he had been invited to advance by the successors of those leaders who had stood in arms to bar the advance of Argyll.

It was calamitous to the national welfare and to Cope's reputation that on quitting the Lowlands he had no choice as to leaving General Guest, eighty-five years of age, in military command, and Colonel Gardiner as senior officer of cavalry.

Notwithstanding the flattering inscription on the tomb of the former in Westminster Abbey, and his being styled by Lord Mahon "an intrepid veteran,"[1] the suspicions as to his fidelity to the house of Hanover appear to be borne out by his continued discouragement of any active opposition to the rebels when they advanced on Edinburgh, by his having been held back (if the account in Chambers's History is to be credited) only by the protests of General Preston from handing over the castle to the Prince, and by his certainly having allowed Charles, in preparation for the invasion of England, to have his Scottish notes exchanged for gold, which had been deposited by the banks for safety in the castle.[2] Regarding Colonel Gardiner, it need only here be remarked that his being at the time "extremely ill"

[1] The '45, p. 40; Chambers's Hist., p. 134 (ed. 1827).
[2] Leaves from the Diary of an Edinburgh Banker, p. 7 *et seq*.

was the reason why Cope did not take him with him instead of Lord Loudon. His age was fifty-seven, a period of life which usually disqualifies an officer from active cavalry duties, but which scarcely merits the term of "venerable" applied to him by Chambers.[1] The epithet would have been fully appropriate had it been given to General Preston, the third officer in high command, who remained in the Lowlands as governor of Edinburgh Castle, and whom the same historian describes as having been then "eighty-six years of age, and so feeble that he could hardly walk. Nevertheless his vigilance was incessant. Once every two hours" during the partial blockade of the castle "he caused himself to be carried round the walls in his arm-chair in order to visit the sentries."

The royal troops marched from Stirling to Crieff on the 20th August, where they were obliged to halt till the 22nd, for the coming up of 100 horse-loads of biscuits. They numbered about 1400 in all, and consisted of Murray's whole regiment, eight companies of Lascell's, five of Lee's, two of Lord John Murray's Highlanders (the Black Watch), and some 50 men of Lord Loudon's regiment, then being recruited. Two companies of Lascell's regiment had been left to strengthen the weak garrison of Edin-

---

[1] Chambers's Hist., p. 134.

burgh Castle, and one of the Black Watch had been sent to guard Inveraray, the home of the Duke of Argyll. For a few days there had been rumours that some disaster had happened to the king's troops near Fort William; but it was not till the 22nd that the truth was known by Cope, although four gentlemen, who had visited his camp on the previous day, must have been fully aware of the facts which had apparently changed the intended political conduct of three of their number. Two of these visitors were the Duke of Atholl and his brother, Lord George Murray. They "came with no more servants than usually attended them."[1] Sir John thus describes the interview with his Grace: "I acquainted the Duke that I had brought 1000 stand of spare arms, and hoped to be joined by a body of his men. The Duke told me that he could not supply the troops with any men, and expressed great concern. I asked his Grace if he did not keep some men in arms as a guard to protect his country from theft: the Duke said he had about twenty or thirty men so employed, who were dispersed at great distances. I begged his Grace to order them to join us, to be a beginning, and to set somewhat of an example to other well-affected clans. The Duke said he would do what he could. Of

[1] Major Caulfield's evidence, Cope's Trial, pp. 142, 181, 16.

these, twelve or thirteen did join us; and after marching a day or two with the army, went home again."

Lord George Murray does not appear to have been present at the conference. He had probably not quite determined on which side he would draw his sword. Like those of his family generally, his own politics had been rather mixed. When a young man and fighting under his brother, the Marquis of Tullibardine, he had been wounded at the action of Glenshiel. Having escaped abroad, he served actively for some years in the Sicilian army. He solicited pardon from King George, which was granted, but his subsequent request for a commission in the British army was refused. His high connections and many accomplishments, however, acquired for him an exalted social position, and his eldest son, who ultimately succeeded to the family dukedom, had recently been commissioned in Lord Loudon's regiment. It has already been stated that the Duke had appointed his brother, Lord George, to aid Cope during his march through the Atholl territory. Doubtless his experienced eye marked the weakness of the force, which, he knew, included all available royal infantry in Scotland, and which he may well have thought might easily be beset and destroyed in some Highland pass. His stay in camp was short, and his promised assistance was never given. After watching events for another fortnight, Lord George joined the Prince at Perth, and at once became virtually the able commander-in-chief of the rebel army. Blame cannot be thrown on him or any other gentleman for choosing at that crisis to stand by the Stuart cause; but his personal espionage in the guise of a friend was an unpleasant feature, and has been judiciously ignored by historians of the Rebellion.

Accompanying the Murray brothers on their visit to the royal camp was the Macdonell of Glengarry, who had, according to Jacobite statements, given a signed promise that he would call out his clan prior to Lochiel's agreeing to join Prince Charles, and whose son, a lieutenant in Lord Loudon's regiment, had five days before, in compliance with that engagement, used a portion of his followers in treacherously waylaying the two companies of the royals near Fort William. The only object of his visit must have been to try for the time to deceive the king's general, and to be able to plead an alibi which would screen him from punishment in the event of a failure of the rising. His caution can scarcely be blamed, but it had in it no touch of romance.

Later on the same day there arrived in the camp Lord Glenorchy with his clansman, Archibald Campbell of Monzie, a lord of the Court of Session, whose home, like that of Lord George Murray, Tullibardine Castle, was near to Crieff.[1] Cope thus summarises the conference and the conclusions which he drew from it. "I acquainted his lordship," he says, "that I had 1000 stand of spare arms; and desired to know what assistance I might depend upon from him. My lord's answer was in substance, that the notice that he had received was so short he could not get his men together. The Earl of Loudon was present at these conferences. We were fully convinced that we had no manner of reason to expect that we were to be joined by any Highlanders on the first part of our march; which so disconcerted us that, if I had been at liberty to act according to my judgment, I would have stopped at Crieff. I declared so to Lord Loudon, who was strongly of the same opinion, but as my orders in the Marquis's letters of the 13th, 15th, and 17th (the two first of which I received at Edinburgh, and the last at Crieff) were positive, I was clearly of opinion that I had nothing left me but to obey." These extracts show that the historian Burton, following the lead of Home and other writers, was scarcely fair to Cope in describing his plan of operation and its motives as follows: "To penetrate with such a force a mountain district inhabited by a large body of hostile armed men, seemed a project bordering on insanity; but the vain

[1] Cope's Trial, p. 17.

expectation was entertained that the well-affected clans would flock to his standard. Cope, in fact, was impatient to march and win laurels by the immediate suppression of the revolt."[1] The plan had really, as has been shown, been heartily supported, if not suggested, by Duncan Forbes and his colleagues.[2] It was sound on military principles as long as the aid of a large body of Highland allies was thought almost certain. When, however, circumstances suddenly altered, and the potentates in the southern Highlands were incapable of fulfilling, or were false to, their recent promises, the Regency became alone responsible for the movement by having repeatedly deprived Cope of any discretionary power, and by having thus rendered it imperative on him to prosecute a course which had become one of unusual peril to his whole force. Though the scheme failed in its main object of at once crushing the insurrection, it was to a considerable extent carried out safely through the General's care and energy, and produced important and beneficial results.

[1] Burton's Hist., vol. ii. p. 443; Home's Works, vol. iii. p. 28.
[2] Cope's Trial, p. 13 *et seq.*

CHAPTER III.

BEFORE leaving Crieff on the 22nd August, Sir John sent back to Stirling all the arms brought for his anticipated Perthshire auxiliaries, except 300 stand, which he carried on in hopes of still obtaining the services of some Macphersons, Grants, or other friendly Highlanders on entering Inverness-shire. The marches at first were necessarily short on account of serious transport difficulties having arisen immediately on entering the Atholl districts.[1] On the very day of leaving Crieff, 100 baggage animals out of those for which "positive assurance" had been given for Lord George Murray "were wanting, and great quantities of provisions were obliged to be left behind, in getting up which to the army (some in the night-time as the horses came up) there was great embezzlement and loss." The country-people would give no information, and occasionally intercepted the correspondence of the

[1] Evidence in Cope's Trial, pp. 23, 24, 45 *et seq.*

force. They seized every opportunity, as the troops were traversing narrow and wooded ravines, to rip up the provision-sacks and destroy, when they could not steal, their contents. Before starting Cope had given orders about taking only necessary luggage. At Tay Bridge (Aberfeldy) on the 23rd, Cope "gave orders again to lighten the baggage, and part was left." This order afforded the only basis for the story of after-writers that he continued to travel with a superfluity of luggage. No possible care could secure the horses of the train, which had to be grazed on the wild unenclosed country. Their drivers rode off with them at night: 200 of them, for instance, thus deserted at Trinifuir on the 24th. The abandoned loads of military stores and provisions had to be left behind in the hands of the stewards of the Duke of Atholl, who promised to send them, "but they never came." Cope had been ridiculed at Edinburgh for providing a drove of black cattle to march with him; but a casual remark in a letter of an officer of the force, written in the following month, states that "without this precaution we had died on the march."[1] Notwithstanding much harassing guard and outpost work, the same witness affirms that "such was the heartiness of the troops for

---

[1] The 'Scots Magazine,' October 1745, p. 477; and 'Gentleman's Magazine,' October 1745, p. 518.

the service, nobody was heard to complain upon the whole march." The daily progress was made as it would have been in an enemy's country. Advance-guards with flanking parties to feel the way and discover any lurking foes, always preceded the main body. These were composed as much as possible—but under trusty officers—of the Highlanders of the Black Watch and Loudon's regiment; and the whole force was so disposed that it could "in three minutes be formed" to receive the attack of an enemy.[1] The numbers of these useful Highlanders, however, quickly "mouldered away" by the nightly desertion of men who carried off their arms with them; so that one company, which had left Stirling "pretty near complete," was in nine days reduced to a muster-roll of fifteen soldiers.[2]

At Dalnacardoch on the 25th August an unexpected visitor, Captain Sweetenham of Guise's regiment, passed through the camp. He had been sent by Cope to assume command of Fort William, but had, when near his destination on 14th August, been kidnapped in an inn by a party of Highlanders. After having been shown off as a prisoner of war at the standard-raising ceremony, he had been dismissed on parole by the Prince, with instructions to describe the scene to

[1] Colonel Whiteford's evidence, Cope's Trial, p. 45.
[2] Cope's Trial, p. 5.

his friends, and with a passport signed "Charles, Pr. Custos Reg."[1] When he left the rebel gathering amounted to about 1400 men, but he had himself met about 400 more marching to join, and on the day of his meeting Sir John he had been informed by Macintosh of Boreland that the rebels now numbered 3000 men. The latter estimate exceeds by nearly one-third that given by the informants of the Lord President; but it has to be borne in mind that these gentlemen were of Jacobite sympathies, and that a constant endeavour was at that time made to minimise the numbers of the insurgents, in order not to excite the alarm of Government. Macintosh had also stated that the rebels proposed to dispute Cope's passage across the mountain range of Corryarrick, which occupied about nine out of the eighteen miles of the last intended march of the royal troops between Garvamore and Fort Augustus. On the 26th Sir John reached Dalwhinnie, thirteen miles from Garvamore.[2] A few miles north of the former place the military road divided into two branches. One led to Inverness by Ruthven, and the other to Garvamore, whence it wended its way for about five miles to the foot of Corryarrick mountain and onwards to the fort. The

[1] Cope's Trial, p. 19; and 'Gentleman's Magazine,' Sept. 1745, p. 496.
[2] Home's Works, vol. iii. p. 23; Cope's Trial, p. 45.

General and several of his officers were personally acquainted with the strongly defensible character of that natural barrier. On its steep and rugged south side, which was intersected by ravines, Wade's road ascended by a succession of seventeen zigzags, traversing the whole breadth of the hill, and presenting many positions which could not be carried against even a few defenders without heavy loss. On its northern slope there were also numerous places where an attacking force, unless excelling in numbers, courage, and agility, would have been placed at hopeless disadvantage; and at one point at least the mere breaking down of a bridge would have rendered the road impassable for wheeled carriages, or even for a single horse.

At Dalwhinnie Cope received an express from the Lord President confirming Captain Sweetenham's account, and cautioning the General "with great concern" against the danger of carrying out his design of proceeding direct to Fort Augustus.[1] Spies sent forward by Sir Patrick Murray of Auchtertyre, who commanded one of the Black Watch companies, now brought back information of the actual occupation of Corryarrick in force by the rebels, and of the placing in concealed batteries, so as to sweep the road at favourable spots, the twenty small field-pieces or swivel-guns

[1] Cope's Trial, p. 20.

which Charles had brought with him in the Doutelle, and which had been seen by the captured officers at Glenfinnan.[1] Cope promptly came to the conclusion that an attack on his part would be "courting the destruction" of his 1400 men. This is the one decision of Sir John during the whole campaign which has not been generally condemned as either rash or weak; but even for it he was reproached by some as "a coward and a traitor."[2] His next step has been more hardly dealt with by many of his critics.[3] Very early on the 27th, before giving orders for the day's march, he summoned a council of war, consisting of his field officers and corps commanders, ten in all. The General, withholding from them his own determination, laid before them his orders from Government, and acquainting them with the reported numbers and situation of the enemy, desired them to give their opinion as to what had best be done. Regarding this council, Sir Walter Scott, echoed by Lord Mahon and others, remarks that such a reference for advice is the favourite refuge of an incapable commander. These councils are not of frequent occurrence in the British service. Yet Clive held one when he meditated a

---

[1] Cope's Trial, p. 44. [2] Ewald's Life of Prince Charles, p. 96.
[3] Cope's Trial, p. 25; Scott's Tales of a Grandfather, vol. ii. p. 272; Mahon's The '45, p. 32.

retreat before the battle of Plassey, and Havelock consulted with his officers after resolving to retire during his first gallant attempt to relieve Lucknow.[1] Neither of these officers has ever been charged with weakness or incapacity. They, like Cope, knew that nothing is more dangerous to success than a loss of confidence in a commanding officer by those serving under him, and that nothing is more certain to dishearten British soldiers than the avoiding of an offered battle, except in a clear case of military necessity. When such a movement, therefore, is contemplated, it may be advisable that officers and men should fully understand that it is caused by no unwillingness to let them fight in a fair field. In calling this council Sir John had no idea of shirking personal responsibility: he thereby adopted the best means of keeping up the trust and spirit of all under his command by letting his officers, and through them his men, know the true cause of his change of plans.

The council was unanimously of opinion that forcing a passage across Corryarrick was "impracticable, without exposing the troops to be cut to pieces or reduced to the necessity of surrendering." They further coincided with the General's already formed conviction as to subsequent operations. There were

[1] Innes's Lucknow and Oude, p. 199.

three courses to be considered. The first was a retreat to Stirling. This plan has since been strongly favoured by the historians Chambers and Burton.[1] But against it there stood the fact that there were in camp provisions for three days only, nearly half of those brought with them having been lost on the march by robbery and by the desertion of the drivers. Experience had shown that no additional supplies could be hoped for on a backward journey. It would, moreover, have been easy for the Prince's men, wholly unencumbered by stores or camp equipage, willingly aided by the inhabitants, and pursuing nearer though rougher routes, to have headed the retiring regulars, and by breaking down bridges to have fixed the starving column in some defile or other locality, where the choice would again lie between destruction and surrender, either of which would have been the signal for a general insurrection in the Highlands and a vast accession to the rebel army. How such an unsound project could have met with the approval of such a clear-headed man as Sir Walter was a mystery, until the recent publication of the Narrative of Murray of Broughton, which was manufactured by him for political purposes some years after the suppression of the Rebellion and his own treachery to the cause.

---

[1] Chambers's Hist., p. 58 ; Burton's Hist., vol. ii. p. 445.

Laboured efforts are therein made to prove Cope's incompetence. From Scott's adopting, with regard to the royal general's conduct on this and other occasions, not only the ideas but also the phraseology of Murray, it is evident that he had a copy of the manuscript before him when he wrote his chapters concerning Prince Charles's enterprise.[1]

[1] Lockhart's Life of Scott, p. 179. Lockhart in his 'Life of Scott' states that he took pleasure in explaining the presence of a saucer—called "Broughton's saucer"—nailed among other Jacobite relics on the wall of his room in his father's house in Edinburgh. Among Mr Scott's clients, as a Writer to the Signet, was Murray of Broughton. During young Scott's boyhood his mother's "curiosity was strongly excited one autumn by the regular appearance, at a certain hour every evening, of a sedan-chair, to deposit a person carefully muffled up in a mantle, who was ushered into her husband's private room, and commonly remained there till long after the usual bedtime. Mr Scott answered her repeated inquiries with a vagueness which irritated the lady's feelings; until one evening, just as she heard the bell ring as for the stranger's chair to carry him off, she made her appearance within the forbidden parlour with a salver in her hand, observing that she thought the gentlemen had sat so long that they would be the better of a dish of tea, and had ventured to bring some for their acceptance. The stranger, a person richly dressed, bowed to the lady, and accepted a cup; but her husband knit his brows and refused very coldly to partake. A moment afterwards the visitor withdrew—and Mr Scott, lifting up the window-sash, took the cup, which had been left empty on the table, and tossed it upon the pavement. The lady exclaimed for her china, but was put to silence by her husband saying, 'I can forgive your little curiosity, madam, but you must pay the penalty. I may admit into my house, as a piece of business, persons wholly unworthy to be treated as guests by my wife. Neither lip of me nor of mine comes after Mr Murray of Broughton's.'" It is not unlikely that Murray consulted his legal adviser regarding the propriety of publishing his Narrative, and left with him a copy of the manuscript. Sir

The second course was for Cope to have formed a standing encampment south of Dalwhinnie. By this means, in the opinion of Sir Walter Scott, who is followed in almost identical words by Lord Mahon and Ewald,[1] he could, "with the full advantage of his artillery," which they omit to state was unmanned by gunners, have checked the advance of the rebels, and have, "cooping them up in their mountains," prevented them from obtaining money and provisions, while he could have drawn his own supplies from Atholl. Sir John would thus, in their view, have forced more numerous and more agile enemies, who, it is admitted, could rely on the sympathies of "all the natives—gentlemen and commoners"—of the district, to hazard a battle which was not obligatory to them on ground of his own choice! But the officers of the council were fully justified in thinking that the results of thus encamping must have been exactly the reverse of these anticipations, and they therefore recommended for adoption the third course, which was to march to Inverness. Burton says of this measure, "A more preposterous military movement was never made."

Walter may have availed himself of this, and in his hasty composition of his historical Tales have relied too strongly on it for facts and arguments.

[1] Tales of a Grandfather, p. 274 ; Mahon's The '45, p. 32 ; Ewald's Life of Prince Charles, p. 96.

Cope, however, wisely considered that he had no option as to carrying it out with all promptitude. By so doing he obeyed, as far as lay in his power, the orders of the Government to secure the chain of fortresses across the Highlands. He had strong reason to believe, with the Regency, that at Inverness he would be joined by such large bodies of well-affected clansmen as would put it in his power not only to seize the lands and herds of the rebels, but also to follow the Prince with increased forces, if he ventured to march towards Edinburgh without first fighting him. Had these hopes been realised, Charles would have been obliged to return northwards, and with diminished numbers do battle on ground chosen by his adversaries.

Cope had a shrewd idea that the sooner he reached the open country about Inverness the better it would be for his interest. But after the council of the 27th, in order to deceive the spies in his camp and the enemy watching his movements from the heights of Corryarrick, he marched his whole force towards the mountain till the van was within four miles of Garvamore and the rear had reached the junction of the roads at Catlaig. The troops were then faced about and proceeded by a forced march to Ruthven on the farther banks of the Spey. They were undisturbed in this movement, partly from the General having ordered a select party of his men with camp-colours flying to advance even nearer Garvamore than the van, and quickly to regain the main body, when time had been allowed the latter to get well ahead on its new route.

This well-planned and effective ruse gave foundation to one of the mass of calumnies which ruined Sir John's credit as a soldier of bravery and intelligence. The 'History of the Rebellion' by Henderson was for more than half a century almost the sole authoritative chronicle of its events. Written in the interest of the Government of the period, and dedicated to George, Prince of Wales, it had already reached its fifth "revised and corrected" edition in 1753. The author professed a knowledge of the trial of Cope in 1746, but he chose to disbelieve the evidence given by the Lord President and a number of other witnesses of unimpeachable honour, and even the signed proceedings of the council of war. "I must be excused," he says, "for writing what I know to be true;"[1] and he wrote that it had been carried at the council to attack the rebels on Corryarrick, but that Sir John, after marching towards them, lost heart, and all at once took "the false step" of moving to Inverness, thus losing an opportunity of either "obtaining an easy

[1] Henderson's Hist., p. 34.

victory or making such a diversion as would have forced the rebels to disband."

On the 28th August, by another forced march through the dangerous pass of Slochmuick, Sir John arrived at Dalrachney, and the next day with his force in good health and spirits reached Inverness, a distance of about fifty miles from Dalwhinnie. Before, however, this was accomplished, the General had two more examples of how little reliance could at that time be placed in the promises of Highland chiefs. Near Dalwhinnie stood Cluny Castle, where resided Ewan Macpherson, eldest son of the head of his clan. He was the writer of the pathetic letters, only eight days old, which have already been alluded to, entreating an advance of royal troops from Stirling to save him from either being burnt out or forced to become a rebel. He was a captain in Lord Loudon's regiment, and duly reported himself to his colonel and to the General on the 26th. He was ordered "to join on the next day with his company; but he never came."[1] Having allowed the king's forces to pass his house on their way to Inverness, he was there by evident arrangement arrested on the following day by a party of Camerons, and carried before the Prince. After a whole month of pitiable hesitation and intrigue, worthy of his father-in-law,

[1] Colonel Whiteford's evidence, Cope's Trial, p. 45.

Lord Lovat, he openly changed sides, "alleging that an angel could not resist the soothing close applications of the rebels."[1] But before yielding to these caresses he seems to have followed the wise example of his friend Lochiel, in obtaining from Charles security for the value of his estate in the event of a failure of the insurrection, and he feebly tried to throw upon Cope the blame of his own dishonourable conduct.

Sir John appears to have felt even more keenly the desertion of the chief of the powerful Grant clan, through whose district the route to Inverness lay. On leaving Dalwhinnie he was met by a relative of that laird, bringing a letter which promised the prompt junction of a considerable body of his men.[2] This spontaneous offer was at once accepted, and the General was assured that 300 at least of the Grant clansmen would be sent to secure the noted pass of Slochmuick, where it was apprehended the royal force might be headed and beset by the rebel and wavering Highlanders.[3] But ere that place was reached another relative of the chief arrived, to say that the whole

---

[1] Culloden Papers, p. 412.   [2] Cope's Trial, p. 30.
[3] In a marginal note on the page of a copy of 'Cope's Trial,' on which these facts are detailed, its original owner, an officer serving with Lee's regiment in the force, remarks: "Grant certainly believed that Sir John Cope was to march by the Corryarrick, which made him send this message. His after-behaviour was of a piece."

clan were required to defend Castle Grant against foes who, however, were invisible. Neither Cluny nor Grant anticipated that their loyal offers would have been so promptly put to the test by a commander whom they believed to be otherwise fully occupied.

On the morning of the 26th August Prince Charles was at Aberchalder, when he heard that Cope, of whose movements he had accurate information, was approaching Dalwhinnie.[1] A council of war was held, which resolved to take possession of the defiles on Corryarrick. "The young forward leader," we are told, "called for his Highland cloaths; and, at tying the lachets of his shoes, he solemnly declared that he would be up with Mr Cope before they were unloosed"—another unfulfilled personal prophecy. Corryarrick was, however, carefully occupied, and while on the mountain on the 27th, news that Cope had taken the Inverness road was brought to Charles by a Macpherson, one of a group of deserters from the king's troops. These as they began to ascend the zigzags were at first taken to be the advance party of an attacking force. The feelings of relief with which the Prince received the tidings that an apparently unavoidable battle was not now to be fought were somewhat in contrast with the sanguine (perhaps *san-*

---

[1] Lockhart Papers, p. 484; Culloden Papers, p. 216.

guinary would have been a more fitting expression) eagerness for combat, admirably ascribed to him by Sir Walter Scott and his other worshippers. "He called," according to Henderson, "for a cask of brandy" (Chambers politely reduces the call to one for a glass), "and taking a glass in his hand said, with a jeering smile, 'Here's a health to Mr Cope.' Usquebaugh was ordered the private men."[1] Poor Scotland is blamed by historians for teaching Charles drinking habits, but Jacobite memoirs prove him to have been an apt pupil.[2]

The Highlanders themselves were sorely "vexed

[1] Henderson's Hist., p. 35.

[2] Hugh Macdonald of Balshar narrates that having in the following June, with Macdonald of Boisdale, entered the hut on the estate of Boisdale in which the Prince was concealed, "the young gentleman" insisted on their sitting up with him that night. They unwillingly consented, and the servant was ordered "to fill the boul; but before we begin with our boul, Boisdale insisted on his being shaved first and then putting on a clean shirt, which he was importuned to do. Burk (the servant) shav'd him. Then we began with our boul, frank and free; as we were turning merry, we were turning more frank and free. We continued this drinking for three days and three nights. He had still the better of us and even of Boisdale himself, notwithstanding his being as able a boulman, I dare say, as any in Scotland" (Lyon in Mourning, vol. ii. p. 97). The good Bishop adds more to prove that Boisdale "was one of the strongest men at a glass in all the Highlands." It is now known from Mr Andrew Lang's researches ('Pickle the Spy,' pp. 13, 27, 29) in the Stuart Papers at Windsor Castle that the Old Chevalier had occasion to remonstrate with his son on account of his drinking habits long before he put foot in Scotland. Even Bishop Forbes admits that Charles would put a bottle of brandy to his lips "without ceremony."

at Cope's escape." "About 600 of them urged the being allowed to follow him, and promised to come up with and give account of his command. But the Prince would not hear of such an attempt. It was with much difficulty they could be prevailed upon to lay aside the thoughts of any such enterprise."[1] Had it been permitted, and had they succeeded in heading the royal troops, there can be little doubt that the clansmen around would have swarmed out to lend a helping hand in the attack, and that Cope would have had a poor chance of ever reaching the open country. On descending from Corryarrick to Garvamore, Charles held another council of war, at which the heads of the clans urged that Sir John's force should be disposed of, and that the other clans should have time to join them before they left the district. But their advices were in vain; the Prince sided with Tullibardine and Murray of Broughton in thinking that the rising of the Atholl men would balance the temporary loss of the wavering clans, and that the glory of capturing the capital of Scotland would more than compensate for a delay in obtaining a possible victory. The march towards Edinburgh was accordingly ordered. But, apparently as a sop to the Highlanders, who were much vexed at what they considered the escape of the royal troops, a detachment sufficient in strength

[1] Lockhart Papers, p. 485; Lyon in Mourning, pp. 208, 294.

to have given much trouble to Cope, had he loitered by the way, was despatched to surprise the redoubt and barracks at Ruthven. It was commanded by Donald Macdonell of Glengarry, now a lieutenant-colonel in the Prince's army, and was accompanied by Dr Archibald Cameron,[1] a brother of Lochiel, and by O'Sullivan, whom Charles had raised to the rank of colonel and appointed to the quartermaster-generalship of his army. The redoubt was held by Sergeant Terence Mulloy and twelve soldiers only. The despatch in which the brave Irishman relates the defence has fortunately been preserved. "There appeared," he says, "above 300 of the enemy, and sent proposals to surrender upon conditions of liberty to carry off bag and baggage. My answer was, I was too old a soldier to surrender a garrison of such strength without bloody noses. They threatened hanging me and my men. I told them I would take my chance. . . . They attacked the foregate and the sally-port, which they attempted to set on fire with some old barrels and other combustibles, which took blaze immediately; but the attempter lost his life by it. I prevented the sally-port taking fire by pouring water over the

[1] Archibald Cameron, informed upon by the double traitor, James Macgregor, son of Rob Roy, was seized in England when on a Jacobite mission in 1752. Among the pleas which he vainly brought forward for his life being spared was his successful efforts in saving the Breadalbane districts from being laid waste.

parapet." Finally the rebels retired, having first been permitted to carry off their own comrades, and leaving several wounded, two mortally, who died in the village. The sergeant only "lost one man, shot through the head by foolishly holding his head too high over the parapet, contrary to order."[1] Cope at once recommended Mulloy for an officer's commission. Æneas Macdonald records that during the fight Colonel "O'Sullivan hid himself in a barn." Full reliance, however, cannot well be placed on the statement, as dissensions had already broken out among the Prince's companions, and Æneas himself was suspected of being a Judas.

Meanwhile, to use the poetic words of Chambers, the Highland "host descended upon the plain, being joined, like one of their own rivers, by accessions of strength at the mouths of all the little glens which they passed"; and the Marquis of Tullibardine had the honour of entertaining his royal master on the 30th of August at his ancestral home, Blair Castle.[2]

Cope, on the other hand, was marching northward, and when nearing Inverness on the 29th August,

[1] Cope's Trial, p. 155; Lyon in Mourning, vol. i. p. 294; H. Walpole's Letters, vol. ii. p. 62.

[2] Chroniclers tell us that Charles saw there for the first time two things which pleased him—a bowling-green and a pine-apple; and that Tullibardine sent a message to his younger brother, the Duke of Atholl, who had fled hastily to London, that he rather liked the alterations made there during his absence.

was met by the Lord President Forbes, whose residence at Culloden stood about four miles to the east of the Highland capital, and who by his wonderful influence and persevering energy had stayed the chiefs of the Macleods, Macleans, Frasers, Grants, Macintoshes, and of many other clans, from as yet joining in the rising. He had not, however, succeeded in persuading any one of them to unite their men with the king's forces, although Cope's advance was a material aid to his other arguments. His partial failure was in a great measure due to the king and Government having refrained from placing at his disposal, till it was too late, money for the payment of private soldiers, and officers' commissions which would have tempted gentlemen of family to have thrown in their lot with the Hanoverian party.[1] In writing to Cope, the President had contrasted his humiliating position with that of Prince Charles, who had begun the campaign by issuing daily pay to his men, and by granting commissions to gentlemen who joined his standard.[2] The unlooked-for condition of local affairs bitterly disappointed Sir John;[3] but, being endowed with the

[1] Culloden Papers, pp. 209, 219, 384.

[2] Forbes ruined his private fortune in the king's service, and, in breach of the most distinct promises, he was never repaid or in any way compensated.

[3] Home's Hist., vol. iii. p. 305.

hardihood which is a necessary factor in the constitution of a good soldier, he was able to write to Lord Milton, the Lord Justice-Clerk, "So much fatigue of body and mind I never before knew; but my health continues good and my spirits do not flag." Not a single man had joined him, and his Highland companies had much "mouldered away by desertion" on his march northward.[1] The Lord President and Cope lost no time in sending expresses to the great northern chiefs, including Lords Lovat, Sutherland, Rea, Fortrose, and Cromartie, the Laird of Grant, and others. The chiefs were called upon at once to send in their men, armed or unarmed. In the latter case it was promised that weapons would be placed in their hands. But the fear of exposing their own country to the fury and resentment of the rebels proved too strong for arguments.[2] Not a man came, except 200 of the Munros, who joined the royal troops the night before they left Inverness, on the condition that they would be discharged at the end of a fortnight, "pretending the necessity of their being at home for their harvest." By the advice of the Lord President Cope, agreed to these terms, as it was deemed well to show the Gordons and other neighbours, who were evincing very strong symptoms of rising for the opposite cause, that they

[1] Cope's Trial, p. 152. [2] Ibid., pp. 33, 47.

would not have it all their own way, even in their own locality. The southward march of the Prince relieved the clans from immediate Jacobite pressure, yet their leaders waited in hopes that events would indicate which party was likely to be victorious before decisively declaring either for the Stuart or the Hanoverian dynasty.

Cope saw the futility of remaining longer in the locality than was necessary to re-supply his commissariat.[1] He had, it is true, been relieved by the Regency of direct responsibility regarding the fate of the Lowlands in his absence, and he had been assured of the arrival of infantry from abroad to support the two regiments of dragoons which had been left in the South; while ships of war secured the waters of the Forth from its estuary to the bridge of Stirling, which was commanded by the castle. These troops, with the aid of local militia and volunteers, who were now ready, on the slightest official encouragement, to assemble and arm in defence of a Protestant Government, ought to have been able, if intelligently commanded, to retard the progress, if they could not fully arrest the advance, of a force of irregular foot soldiers. But Cope knew the inefficiency of the commanders in the Lowlands, and that his request

[1] Cope's Trial, pp. 130, 128.

for the despatch of capable officers had not met with compliance. The loyalty of the Provost of Edinburgh, then a powerful functionary, was very doubtful. Cope was anxious too that, if the serious legal penalties involved in the assembly in arms even of loyal subjects to resist the rebels could not at once be removed on the king's authority, they should be exempt from the possible consequences of such patriotic action. He therefore, on the 31st of August, unaware that on that very day King George had arrived in London, risked incurring the displeasure of many high in rank and influence by addressing in a private letter the following appeal to Lord Milton : " General Guest will show you my letter to him. I, from the beginning, thought the affair serious ; and sorry I am that I was not mistaken : indeed, my Lord, it is serious. I know your activity and ability in business — the whole is at stake — exert your authority — lengths must be gone ; and rules and common course of business must yield to the necessity of the times, or it may be too late. . . . No man could have believed that not one man would take arms [here] in our favour, or show countenance to us ; but so it is. I can say no more."[1] In a postscript he adds, " Pray attend and give assistance to Guest."

[1] Home's Hist., vol. iii. p. 305.

This letter proves that Sir John was not, as is often charged, a formal red-tapist, and is in marked contrast with the piteous note sent to the same dignitary by General Guest on his receipt of Cope's despatch :—

"MY DEAR LORD,—I never had more need of your advice. For God's sake come to, my dear Lord, your most humble servant,   JOS. GUEST."

Unreasonable expectations had been universally formed as to the results of the northern march, and Sir John Cope had to bear the brunt of the disappointment caused by its failure. Lord Tweeddale himself was the blindest of the optimists. On the 17th of August he expressed to Craigie, the Lord Advocate, his private doubts as to Prince Charles having ever landed in Scotland; and even on the 24th, in writing to Lord Milton, he still doubted the fact.[1] On the latter date he wrote to the Lord President, "There have been transmitted to me from Sir John Cope and others of his Majesty's servants in Scotland several pieces of intelligence so very extraordinary that they did not gain the least credit with me;" and after untruly blaming the General for "unneces-

---

[1] Omond's Lord Advocates; Home's Hist., vol. iii. p. 277; Culloden Papers, p. 385.

sary delay" in marching, he adds, " I can have no notion but that Sir John, even with the few forces he has, keeping them in a body, and going directly to the place pointed out" (the line of forts), "will be able to quell very soon any insurrections that may have happened or may happen." So little did the Secretary for Scotland realise the true state of political feeling in the North that he wrote a letter to Cope, dated 7th September, when the General was well out of the district, and transmitted for the first time the king's permission for him to act freely in his Majesty's service, as he alone was in a position to judge what was best to be done. He could not refrain from suggesting that Sir John should send some of "the many well-affected clans" into the country of the rebels to drive off their black cattle and sheep, and others to secure the passes and prevent the return of the rebels to their harried homes. He wrote confidently, too, of the two regiments of dragoons with the Dutch regiment being able to retard the progress of the rebels till Cope's forces came up with them.[1] Most of the British public fully shared in these too sanguine anticipations, and attributed their non-fulfilment entirely to the shortcomings and bad conduct of the luckless General,

[1] Cope's Trial, p. 135.

who was not even credited with having prevented thousands of ready warriors from joining the Prince, and thereby swelling his force into a formidable army. The effect produced by the arrival of the royal troops on the chief of the Frasers, for example, is recorded in a letter from Lord Lovat to "the Laird of Lochiel," who was with the Prince. He writes :—

"I fear you have been rash in going out ere affairs were ripe. The Elector's General Cope is in your rear, hanging at your tail with 3000 men—such as we have not seen since Dundee's affair—and we have no force to meet him. If the Macphersons would take the field, I would bring out my lads to help the work, and 'twixt the twa we might cause Cope to keep his Xmas heir; bot only Cluny is earnest in the cause, and my Lord Advocate [Craigie] plays at cat-and-mouse with me; but times may change, and I may bring him to the Saint Johnstoun's tippet.[1] Meantime look to yourselves, for ye may expect many a sour face and sharp weapon in the south. I'll aid you what I can, but my prayers are all I can give at present. My service to the Prince, but I wish he had not come heir soe empty-handed; sillar would

[1] St Johnstoun was the patron saint of Perth, which was called St John's Town, and the expression above used means death by hanging.

go a long way in the Highlands. I send this be Ewan Fraser, whom I have charged to give it to yourself, for, were Duncan [the Lord President] to find it, it would be my head to an onion.—Farewell. Yʳ faithfull friend,   LOVAT."[1]

Sir John Cope now felt it to be his first duty to place his own troops in fighting contact with those of the Prince. He knew, as has been said, that if he tried to attack them by returning over the road which he had already traversed, his force, unsupported by the Highlanders, would be destroyed. Had it been feasible, he would have preferred this means of attack. The coast road by Aberdeen, Dundee, and the estuary of the Tay was no doubt still partially open, and offered a second means of following and perhaps heading the rebels; but it was longer, and the Prince from his proximity to that river could now command all the boats upon it, and perhaps frustrate a crossing. Under these circumstances Cope ably devised and carried out a third plan. He sent orders by Captain Rogers,[2] who

---

[1] Tales of a Grandfather, vol. ii. p. 291.

[2] Regarding this despatch-bearer a curious manuscript note by an officer of his own (Lee's) regiment runs thus: "A general should know those he sends with orders. Captain Rogers, when sent to General Guest" (he had embarked at Inverness), "was put on shore at Banff, and there told to Provost Abernethie what he was going about. The Provost put the

was shortly afterwards killed at the battle of Prestonpans, to General Guest, directing him to despatch to Aberdeen transports sufficient for his force. He himself determined, as soon as bread for the journey was available, to march to that port, a distance of 130 miles, and there to embark for Leith. The sea voyage was one of only ninety miles, and he calculated that, with ordinary good fortune, he would reach his destination before the Prince. Sir John accordingly sent another good officer, Colonel Whiteford, to make shipping arrangements at Aberdeen, and marched from Inverness on the 4th September, taking with him a second experienced company of Guise's regiment. He was aware that the Prince possessed some twenty swivel-guns, so he added to his small artillery train two more $1\frac{1}{2}$-pounder galloper guns and two small cohorn mortars. He had reasonable hopes of being met on landing in the Forth by the artillerymen, whom he had some time before requested the Government to send from London, and who would have rendered efficient all his little pieces of ordnance. In case of running short of provisions on land, the General hired a vessel with meal on board,

Jacobites on making the most of his intelligence, by endeavouring to alarm the men with a design to ship them to Cape Britain." Cape Breton in Nova Scotia, which had been recently taken from the French, is doubtless meant.

which, under convoy of the sloop of war, Happy Janet, kept sailing along the coast while the soldiers proceeded by land. Aberdeen was reached by Wednesday the 11th, the march having been accomplished in eight days without a halt having been made *en route*. Colonel Whiteford records that Sir John had taken the greatest care of his troops on the march, and "had kept such exact discipline that no outrage had been committed by the soldiers, nor was there one complaint from his going forth to his return." At Aberdeen he received a letter from Lord Tweeddale, dated 7th September, which stated: "It is likewise hoped that the two regiments of dragoons in the low country on this side of the Forth, with the Dutch regiment, which may by this time be arrived at Leith, will be able to retard the progress of the rebels till you come up with them with your forces; and I must observe to you, by the by, that none of our intelligence makes them to be at most above 2500 strong."[1]

The transports arrived at Aberdeen at the same time as the force, but did not get into the harbour till the 12th. Water, provisions, and stores were at once placed on board. The vessels would have sailed on the 14th, had an adverse wind not prevented their departure till Sunday, the 15th, when the little army was embarked.

[1] Cope's Trial, p. 135.

Owing to light breezes and calms, the fleet was not off the Isle of May, at the mouth of the Forth, till the afternoon of Monday. Three or four hours of fair wind would now have easily taken them to Leith in time to save Edinburgh from the rebels, who, as we shall see, were then at its gates. Unfortunately for Cope, a scant breeze blew directly out of the Firth and compelled him to make for Dunbar and land his forces on Tuesday the 17th at that port, twenty-seven miles from Edinburgh. He then learned that on that very morning, in consequence of the almost incredible failures in duty on the part of the officers in command, the general absence of energy on the part of the "king's servants," and the adroit treachery of the Provost, the capital had been surrendered without opposition to Prince Charles.

It has been mentioned that the Prince arrived at Blair Castle on the 30th of August. "The morning after his arrival," to quote from Chambers, "he reviewed his troops. Some whom he had lately seen around him being now wanting, he despatched a few of his officers to bring them forward to Blair, when it was found that their only reason for lingering behind was that they had been denied the satisfaction of pursuing General Cope"![1] But probably a stronger

[1] Chambers's Hist., p. 64.

motive for their disobedience lay in an instinctive dread that in their absence their own homes would be pillaged by the royal soldiers, or by neighbours to whom such an opportunity of revenge might be only too tempting. During the delay of two days thus caused, Charles was joined by Lord Nairn, who had been pardoned for his share in the Rebellion of 1715, and by several gentlemen of the county. Other landed proprietors fled at his approach. On the 2nd September he reached Dunkeld, another seat of the Atholl family, where a banquet was given in his honour by Tullibardine, who had assumed the dukedom. The 'History of the Rebellion' by Chambers, though written by a warm partisan of the Stuarts, is described by Lord Mahon as "very full and exact."[1] Yet while professing to quote from the contemporary historian (Henderson), Chambers not only gives a wrong place and date to the supper at Dunkeld, but gives a different description of the demeanour of the Prince from that furnished by the original author. Chambers writes that Charles "exerted himself to appear cheerful, though the anxiety arising from his circumstances occasionally drew a shade of thoughtfulness over his otherwise sprightly features." But Henderson's real

---

[1] Mahon's The '45, p. 15; Chambers's Hist., p. 64; Henderson's Hist., p. 36.

words were, "The adventurer did all in his power to appear cheerful notwithstanding he was generally thought dull and morose." He was, in fact, already showing that nature had not endowed him with the enduring resolution which alone could carry him through his foolhardy enterprise. Lovat, Macleod, Sir Andrew Macdonald, and others on whom he had depended as the mainstays of his undertaking, still declined to join his standard, while the few chiefs who had staked their lives in his cause had ventured to place a value on their services and loyalty which he thought he had a divine right to command gratuitously.

During his southern march further uneasiness was caused to the Prince by the keen desire displayed by the Camerons and Macdonalds to ravage the lands lying to the west of their route, belonging to the vassals of the Earl of Breadalbane. Many old feud-wrongs, culminating in the massacre of Glencoe, were still unavenged; and it needed all the influence possessed by Lochiel and his brother, Dr Archibald Cameron, to restrain the passions of their followers. Any such outbreak would at that time have had a baneful effect upon the Stuart cause, and would certainly have destroyed the hope still cherished, slightly by Charles and more strongly by his father, of obtaining the support of both the Duke of Argyll and the Earl of Breadalbane, the chiefs of the powerful Campbell clan. In the Rebellion of 1715 the Duke of the period had commanded the king's forces, while the Earl's followers had furnished a strong contingent to the rebel army.[1] In the present struggle neither of the chiefs had as yet been forward in aiding the existing Government. Lord Glenorchy, the Earl's eldest son, had not given his promised help to Cope, while the Earl's own sympathies were shortly afterwards shown by his intimacy with Murray of Broughton and the Prince at Holyrood, and also by his probable knowledge of the various interventions, not unfriendly to Charles, on the part of General Guest, then commanding in Edinburgh Castle.

On the evening of the 4th September Charles made his public entry into Perth, where his father had already been proclaimed as king and he himself as regent. It is recorded by Chambers that the horse ridden by him on this occasion "was the first good horse mounted by the Prince in Scotland,"[2] and that it had been presented to him by Macdonald of Tiendrish, now a major in the rebel army. But the polite

[1] Memoir of Colonel J. Cameron of Fassiefern, pp. 15, 104; Letter from Charles to his father, Ewald's Life of Prince Charles, p. 104; Diary of an Edinburgh Banker, p. 3 *et seq.*; Wood's Peerage of Scotland, vol. i. p. 239; D. Murray Rose in 'Scotsman,' 16th March 1896.

[2] Lyon in Mourning, vol. i. p. 207.

author does not add that the major had looted the animal from the wounded Captain Scott, "son of Scotstarvet," who had commanded the two companies of royal recruits caught in the ambuscade on the 16th of August. A halt of a whole week was made at Perth, during which the exhausted rebel cash-chest was somewhat replenished by money exactions made on that town and on Dundee, Montrose, and neighbouring places, and also by voluntary contributions sent by partisans in Edinburgh. The force was also considerably reinforced. Although Chambers states that Tullibardine had great difficulty in raising his tenants, he affirms that Atholl men "now poured themselves into the tide of insurrection."[1] Robertson of Struan, Oliphant of Gask, Lord Ogilvie, and the two Drummonds, the titular Duke of Perth, and Lord Strathallan,[2] were among the gentlemen who now brought in contingents of not always very willing followers.[3]

[1] Chambers's Hist., p. 68; Home's Hist., p. 44.
[2] Lord Strathallan, true to the motto of his branch of the family, "Prius quam fidem fallere," fell at Culloden. The Duke of Perth, whose older motto, "Gang warily," was not so appropriate, escaped from the battle, but died shortly after on his passage to France, worn out with fatigue and anxiety.
[3] An amusing instance of alleged pressure into rebellion is given in a petition, printed in the 'Scottish Antiquary' for July 1896, from William Fleming to the Secretary of State in 1746. Fleming had been a servant

No family had been more truly loyal to the Stuarts in their recent misfortunes than that of the Duke of Perth. His grandfather, the Chancellor of Scotland, had followed James VII. in exile to France; and his father, before taking part in the Rebellion in 1715, had formally conveyed his estates to his son the present Duke, then an infant of only three months old.[1] The domains were thus saved from forfeiture after that rising. The Government, on hearing the news of the present outbreak, and being assured of the Duke's connection with it, authorised his capture by a disgraceful stratagem. His neighbour and friend, Sir Patrick Murray of Auchtertyre, who commanded the companies of the Black Watch at Crieff, utilised his Grace's hospitality by arranging that he and another officer, Campbell of Inverawe, should dine at Drummond Castle, the Duke's house, on July 26. During the repast the wood about the house was surrounded by their soldiers, and towards its conclusion Sir

to the reigning Duke of Atholl, when in August 1745 "the person commonly called the Marquis of Tullibardine came with a body of rebels, who seized your petitioner," and "proposed that he must either enlist as a common soldier in the service of the Pretender or enter into the Marquis's service as his gentleman, and your petitioner being under that necessity agreed to serve the Marquis as his gentleman." He was in attendance as such when that unfortunate nobleman, worn out with illness during his attempted flight to the west coast after Culloden, surrendered to his connection, Buchan of Drumakill, on the 27th April 1746.

[1] Wood's Peerage of Scotland, vol. ii. p. 364.

Patrick produced a warrant for arresting his host. The Duke saw that resistance was useless, and, to quote the words of Bishop Forbes, "commanded his temper very well. He told them he would step into the closet, which was in the room where they were sitting, and get himself ready. To this they agreed, as they thought he could not get out of the room. He went into the closet, and gently locking the door, slipt down a pair of backstairs which came to it, and got into the wood joining his gardens with much difficulty."[1] He crawled on his hands and knees through thorns and briers, and "lay squat in a dry ditch" till the cordon of soldiers had gone. The Duke not returning, the Highland officers, after finding the door of the closet locked, had summoned the servants, and had been assured by them that their master had ridden away in a great hurry.[2]

[1] Lyon in Mourning, vol. i. p. 291.
[2] On the 21st September following, after the battle at Prestonpans, Sir Patrick Murray, who with his followers—Highlanders—had been posted by Cope at Cockenzie House, half a mile from the scene of action, surrendered without firing a shot to Lord George Murray and Lochiel; and—again to quote from Bishop Forbes—"the Duke of Perth came up to him, and asking him how he did, spoke these words very kindly, 'Sir Petie, I am to dine with you to-night.'"

The mother of the Duke, Lady Jean, a zealous Roman Catholic and the only daughter of the first Duke of Gordon, was "for her support to the rebels committed prisoner to Edinburgh Castle, 11th February, and liberated on bail 17th November 1746" (Wood's Peerage, vol. ii. p. 364).

An even more important addition to the strength of the insurgents than that of this brave and amiable nobleman was gained at this juncture by the arrival of Lord George Murray, the brother of the Marquis of Tullibardine, and of the Duke of Atholl, whose previous changes of adherence, and whose visit to Cope's camp as commissariat provider to the royal troops, have already been noticed. His advent is thus described by Henderson : "Lord George, being admitted to his brother's presence, fell on his knee before him, and proferred his service; the Marquis signified his distrust, though he accepted of it, on which Lord George bound himself with a curse that he would be faithful and true. This being over and a very sumptuous dinner prepared, as Lord George was a great epicure, though very strong and courageous, he set out directly for the Pretender's quarters, where he was no sooner arrived than he was made lieutenant-general of the king's army." The Duke of Perth was nominated to the same rank. But Lord George was the abler and older of the pair, and besides possessing previous campaigning experience, he was gifted with a natural military genius. These advantages and the trust reposed in him by the Scottish leaders caused him to become at once practically the rebel commander-in-chief. His superior influence excited the jealousy of the Duke of Perth, who perhaps had a suspicion that Lord George Murray had not been without some knowledge of the recent attempted arrest. The Duke was supported both by Secretary Murray, who dreaded the power which the master-mind of his namesake was likely to exercise in the counsels of the Prince, and by the Irish officers, whose qualifications Lord George Murray rather too openly despised. The dissensions thus arising were a source of weakness, which lasted to the close of the enterprise.

The 'Caledonian Mercury,' the Jacobite Edinburgh paper of the time, records that after his arrival at Perth "the Young Chevalier gets up every morning before the sun to review his people." He and his Irish and French officers busied themselves, with more zeal than knowledge or discretion, in trying to instil into the Gaelic-speaking Highlanders the minutiæ of regular drill—a process always trying to the tempers of the teachers and the taught. "His men," according to Henderson,[1] "were very backward in learning their exercise, perhaps through their want of the English language, and he some-

[1] Henderson's Hist., p. 37; Tales of a Grandfather, vol. ii. p. 284; Chambers's Hist., p. 70.

times, though in a low tone, called them '*his staigs*.'"[1]

Lord George did good service to the Prince by advising him, with reference to his Highland followers, to trust to their own mode of fighting, rather than to attempt to instruct them in any more scientific manœuvres. They already knew how to march in sections of three men abreast, and by simply turning to the right or left to form a line of battle. From such a line they could also break into masses of columns, and experience had often proved to them that a rapid attack in this more solid formation was successful against a mere line of infantry, unless the charge was stopped by a steady fire of artillery or musketry. The energy and personal influence of Lord George were also most useful in organising the various bodies of clansmen into distinct regiments and brigades. But what he himself places in the forefront of his good deeds were his services with regard to provisions—a topic

---

[1] This is the word which in the Scottish language is applied to unbroken colts—animals rather notorious for intractability and clumsy action. Chambers, himself a Lowland Scot, while giving the contemporary historian as his authority, thus amusingly travesties the foregoing quotation. "At a review," he says, "Charles was observed to smile occasionally at the awkwardness of the general behaviour of his men: at the same time he complimented their agility and wild elegance by calling them *his stags*."

which, Mr Chambers apologetically remarks, "makes but a poor appearance in a romantic narrative."[1] Lord George writes: "As I had formerly known something of a Highland army, the first thing I did was to advise the Prince to endeavour to get proper people for provisors and commissaries, for otherwise there would be no keeping the men together, and that they would straggle through the whole country upon their marches, if it was left to them to find provisions; from which, beside the inconveniency of irregular marches and much time lost, great abuses would be committed, which above all things we were to avoid. I got many of the men to make small knapsacks of sacken before we left Perth, to carry a peck of meal upon each occasion, and I caused take as many threepenny loaves as would be three days' bread to our small army, which was carried in carts. I sent about 1000 of these knapsacks to Crieff to meet the men that were coming from Atholl" under the Marquis of Tullibardine. In his letter to this brother on Saturday, 7th September, apprehensive that 1000 would not suffice, he said: "Cost what it will, there must be pocks made for each man. Buy linen, harn, or anything, for these pocks are of absolute

---

[1] Chambers's Hist., p. 70; Jacobite Memoirs, p. 30.

necessity—nothing can be done without them." His foresight was soon justified, for he himself had to record that as soon as the sport-loving and hungry Highlanders entered the pasture-lands of the Lowlands, they "committed abuses in taking and shooting sheep, and the Duke of Perth and other officers rode about and did all in their power to prevent it, and promised satisfaction to the country-people."

CHAPTER IV.

WHILE the Prince's force was thus being reinforced and organised, the unlooked-for intelligence arrived that Cope had marched from Inverness, and had arranged to embark at Aberdeen for Leith. It was at once seen that if Cope succeeded in getting first to Edinburgh, all hope of gaining the capital without a doubtful contest would be gone; that the supporters of Government, who were now awakening to a sense of real danger, would be much encouraged by his presence and activity; while the confidence of the Jacobites would be in proportion lowered. It has been mentioned that on Wednesday, 11th September, Sir John reached Aberdeen, and that, had the winds been favourable, he could easily have arrived at his destination in two days thereafter. Yet it was not till that Wednesday that the preparations of Charles were sufficiently advanced to enable him to set out for Dunblane, the first stage on his march of eighty miles to the capital. The chances seemed to be against him in the race, and they were further diminished by his having to start—to use the words of a friendly historian, Sir Walter Scott—with only "the vanguard of his army, or rather detachments of the best men of every clan. It was found very difficult to remove the others from the good quarters and provisions of Perth."[1] The numbers of the body who first quitted Perth were reported by Captain Vere, an English officer and eyewitness, to have been about 2000.[2] On the morning of this day, the 11th, the Prince walked to Scone, a distance of about two miles from Perth, where so many of his ancestors had been crowned;[3] and afterwards, we are told by one of his fellow-passengers in the Doutelle, he took a second breakfast at the seat of Oliphant of Gask,[4]

[1] Scott's Tales of a Grandfather, vol. ii. p. 301.

[2] Ewald's Life of Prince Charles, p. 105, quoting State Papers, Scotland, September 12, 1745.

[3] Lyon in Mourning, vol. i. p. 209.

[4] There are two interesting records of this visit to Gask. One was gathered from tradition by Mr Chambers. The Prince had been told that the auld laird, usually "sae canty, kind, and crouse," was doing political harm by an over-zealous act. Incensed at some of his tenants having refused to "fight for Charlie," he had laid a legal arrestment upon their fields, which prevented them from cutting their crops or grazing their starving cattle. Charles, on observing the corn hanging dead ripe, leaped from the saddle, and gathering some ears, gave them to his horse, exclaiming, "This will never do." He then told those around him that he had thus broken Gask's inhibition, and that the farmers might now,

who has been called "the staunchest Jacobite in Scotland," and dined at Tullibardine, the home of Lord George Murray. A halt at Dunkeld on the 12th was compulsory to enable the mass of his men who had loitered behind to rejoin. There he was joined by a second party of Macdonalds of Glencoe, and by the retainers of the chief of the Macgregors under James, the eldest son of Rob Roy. A detachment of some 300 men was sent forward on that day to light fires on the rising grounds opposite Stirling, and thus occupy the attention of the garrison. On the next day, Friday, this party advanced as if it intended to force a passage across the bridge, which had been in parts broken down to impede such an attack; and General Blakeney, who had recently arrived from London to assume local command, directed an innocuous fire to be opened on them by a portion of Gardiner's dragoons from the south side of the Forth.[1] Meanwhile the Prince with his main body, probably about 5000 men in strength,

upon his authority, put the produce of their fields to its proper use. The second record is in the charming song by the Lady Nairne, the granddaughter of "The auld laird," which states that

"the leddy too, sae genty,
There sheltered Scotland's heir,
And clipt a lock wi' her ain hand
Frae his lang yellow hair."

[1] Caledonian Mercury, 16th September 1745.

had marched through Doune to the ford at Frew, seven miles above Stirling, where, wrote one of his officers, "we expected to have been opposed by the dragoons, who had encamped in the park at Stirling, and who, we heard, had threatened to cut us to pieces if we attempted to cross the water." These troops had, however, "galloped away in a great hurry, and lay that night at Falkirk," ten miles distant from the road to Edinburgh.[1] Their absence must have given a sense of relief; for the clansmen, brave though they were, retained their dread of cavalry on the open ground. They knew that no foot soldiers, unless they were in solid formation and suitably armed, could stand up before a charge of horsemen. Some now in their ranks had been at the battle of Sheriffmuir, the scene of which was near their last camping-ground, and had witnessed the disastrous effects upon their clan-columns of such onsets of the dragoons of the then Duke of Argyll. But now no regular soldier or volunteer was within sight to dispute the passage. From a lengthened drought the stream flowed in a gentle current only knee-deep, and the historians inform us that "the adventurer's heart was screwed up to every hazard." Coming to the brink of the river, he "drew his sword,

[1] Stuart Papers, p. 487.

flourished it in the air, and pointing to the other side, walked into the stream with an air of resolution."¹ His advent had been fully expected, and a banquet in his honour awaited him at Leckie House, about a mile from the ford. The laird himself, Mr Moir, had been seized during the previous night by a party of dragoons, who considerately spared the viands, and, as recorded by a grateful guest, "the Prince and his followers were received in the most hospitable manner, as well as any other of our friends who followed soon after."² His little army bivouacked in peace on the moor of Touch during the night.

A rougher welcome would have been given to Charles on the south side of the Forth had not the king, the Secretary of State for Scotland, and two of the military commanders, General Guest and Colonel Gardiner, crushed every effort towards practical resistance. The Lowlanders had become thoroughly alarmed at the now apparent danger alike to their religious and civil liberty, should a Prince, who still preferred the Roman Catholic faith, become their ruler.

¹ Chambers's Hist., p. 82.
² Chambers states that the Prince slept in Bannockburn House on the night of the 17th; but that house is to the south-east of Stirling, and he would not have slept so far from his men. He spent the night probably in Touch House, where lived Elizabeth Seton, heiress of Touch, who had married Patterson's son, Hugh.

Some among them recollected that his grandfather had found a personal enjoyment in witnessing the persecutions and tortures inflicted upon martyrs whose only crime was their refusal of Episcopacy. Their feelings at this crisis may be gathered from the writings of Lord Milton. He wrote as follows to the Marquis of Tweeddale: " There was yesterday a meeting at my house, where the Lord Advocate, the Provost, some other of the Council, and well-affected inhabitants, were deliberating about the means to raise some men, *by authority of the Crown*, for the protection of this place in case of danger, until effectual means were found to suppress the rebels. I was glad to see a rising zeal for the support of his Majesty's Government. . . . I have a letter from the magistrates of Glasgow, much to the same purpose, desiring arms and ammunition, which I communicated to the Lord Advocate and General Guest, but they did not seem to think themselves empowered to give any directions in the matter." This despatch was laid before the king, who had arrived in London on the 30th. He declined to give "any particular orders," but directed Lord Tweeddale to add, " You may expect at Leith with the first fair wind a battalion of Swiss from Holland, and more will immediately follow should there be occasion for them." On September 6, after receiving Sir John Cope's appeal, which has already been mentioned, for immediate action in raising troops, Lord Milton again wrote, stating, among other intelligence, that, in defiance of the Act of Parliament, and on his own responsibility, " Mr Napier, the Sheriff of Stirling, had raised 100 men, to be a night-watch, and save the dragoons from being harassed, particularly with false alarms; and that the people on the south side of Forth offer to guard the passes and fords of the river, provided they be supplied with arms, &c. Offers of a like nature came from Glasgow, Aberdeen, and the shires of Dumbarton, Dumfries, and Stirling, which I laid before the Lord Advocate; and it's a pity there is no power or authority here, properly supported, to employ the friends of Government, and put the nation in a posture of defence." Next day the Lord Justice-Clerk again wrote, sending more applications from other counties and towns for arms and ammunition, and adding: "It is with difficulty I can walk the streets of Edinburgh from the attacks, not of the enemies of Government, but from the attacks of its most zealous friends, asking why the well-affected to the present happy establishment are not armed and properly supported, and empowered in a legal way for the defence of his Majesty's person and support of his Government, and the preservation of our religion, liberty, and property?

Although I have written often on the subject, I am sorry I have not been empowered to say anything satisfactory to so faithful subjects. Meantime, I can assure your lordship I do all I can to encourage and keep alive so laudable a zeal for his Majesty's service, as far as apologies for the time past, and giving them better hopes in time to come, will go; but my credit will soon be exhausted, unless some salutary measures be soon laid down, or that a kind Providence once more interpose in our behalf." These appeals were laid before the king on the 11th, and Lord Tweeddale was directed to reply that warrants had been sent for the cities of Glasgow and Aberdeen authorising the levying of men; but that the supply of arms and ammunition to these men "must depend on his Majesty's pleasure, who will judge if it be expedient for his service." But the applications from counties were to be subject to a different and future consideration, and the Marquis added that if Lord Milton "would condescend" to state particularly the powers and authorities desired, "his Majesty could determine whether it was convenient for the service, or indeed useful, to grant such powers at this critical juncture." It may be here remarked that on the 13th of September letters were sent by Government, directing the lord lieutenants of counties in England and Wales to call out the militia, but no such orders were issued to Scotland, which was apparently distrusted by his Majesty. The letter of the Marquis thus closes: "As the wind is fair, part of the Dutch troops will, I hope, be arrived at Leith before this can reach you. More will immediately follow, and I make not the least doubt that in a very little time those who have favoured the desperate attempt of a Popish Pretender will soon vanish, and their persons meet the fate they deserve." Lord Milton began a lengthy and indignant reply from Edinburgh, but before it was finished he had been obliged to fly for his personal safety from the capital. British, Swiss, and Dutch troops had in succession been promised by Lord Tweeddale for immediate service in the Lowlands. The king had at Helvoit Sluys on the 27th of August conferred with leaders of his army in Flanders, and it was in his power to have directed to Leith a portion of the troops at his disposal.[1] He was then fully aware of the presence of Prince Charles and of the rising in Scotland. Yet to that country he ordered only one regiment of Dutch, which did not arrive at Berwick till the 23rd of September; while on the 17th seven battalions of foreign troops, and on the 23rd of September three battalions of Foot Guards and seven regiments of British infantry,

[1] Gentleman's Magazine for 1745, p. 447.

had landed in the Thames. It is beyond the scope of this narrative to inquire into the probable reasons which guided his Majesty's judgment. The fact, however, remains, that the Rebellion, as it then stood, could easily have been crushed by using on the spot a portion of this mass of experienced soldiers.

The officer whose duty it now was to stop or impede the progress towards Edinburgh of the Prince's force was Colonel Gardiner. Sir Walter Scott records the general estimation in which he was held when he states that "he was celebrated for his private worth, his bravery, and his devotional character."[1] Sprung from a military family, he had been a soldier from boyhood. Born in 1688 near Linlithgow, and educated there, the localities were familiar to him. With his tall and handsome person, his winning manners, his fine horsemanship, and with a voice strong or gentle as he chose to tone it, he had been the *beau idéal* of an officer. When only eighteen years of age he had been left grievously wounded on the field of Ramillies. In his later career he benefited by the steady patronage of the Earl of Stair, on whose ambassadorial staff he had served for many years. It was while at Paris that he was reclaimed from a morally loose life in the year

---

[1] Tales of a Grandfather, vol. ii. p. 308.

1719 by what he regarded as a miraculous vision.[1] It would be almost irreverent to dwell on this private episode, were it not that some of its results appear to have had a great influence in the campaign under consideration. A reputation for holding deep religious principles has fortunately in our army always enhanced the power of an officer, provided that the religious convictions of the men are not injudiciously interfered with, and provided also that it be accompanied by a proved willingness to head them bravely on every opportunity of a fair fight. Unhappily with Gardiner's altered life there came a somewhat narrowing creed. He tolerated no deviation from his own views of a correct life; he believed that future retribution awaited all those who so deviated; and he lost no chance of enforcing this conviction to an extent and in a manner that would be incredible if it were not vouched for by "his affectionate friend and biographer," Dr Doddridge. That writer relates as a favourable instance of his conduct in after-years that, when his regiment was encamped near Leicester, Gardiner himself lodging in the town, "the Colonel went incognito to the camp in the middle of the night. One of the sentinels then on duty had abandoned his post, and on being seized, broke into some oaths and execrations against those

[1] Doddridge's Life of Gardiner, p. 32; Carlyle's Autobiography, p. 16.

that had discovered him—a crime of which the Colonel had the greatest abhorrence. The man appeared much ashamed and concerned for what he had done." (Doubtless when he discovered that his commanding officer was the amateur detective.) "But the Colonel ordered him to be brought early the next morning to his own quarters, where he had prepared a piquet on which he appointed him a private sort of penance." A military author thus describes this "penance." The man to be picketed was "mounted on a block or stool, while his right hand was being secured at its full extent to a ring that had previously been driven into the wall or into a tall post. Close to this point were two stumps bluntly pointed at the top and fixed firmly in the ground. The block or stool was then removed from under him, and the pointed stumps were substituted as the only rests for his feet. It is only after a personal trial that the painful nature of it can be appreciated, the aching in the feet and wrists becoming intolerable after a few minutes."[1] The reverend doctor states that, while Gardiner's victim was thus being tortured, the Colonel "discoursed with him seriously and tenderly upon the evils and aggravations" (evidently the swearing) "of his fault, admonished him of the divine displeasure, and urged him to argue, from

---

[1] Colonel Walton's Hist. of the British Army, p. 571.

the pain which he then felt, how infinitely more dreadful it must be to 'fall into the hands of the living God,' and indeed to meet the terrors of that damnation which he had been accustomed to call on himself and his companions."

In 1743, while serving in Flanders, he was promoted to the colonelcy of his regiment, which was quartered at Linlithgow. On his journey homewards at Ghent he was prostrated by a severe attack of fever; and this, combined with the effects of a previous bad fall, probably damaged his mental as well as his bodily health. The idea of his own speedy death was never out of his mind, and though he constantly expressed a longing for it in his own case, he was shocked at the fate which a similar event would, according to his sincere conviction, bring upon his soldiers and others whom he cared for, and who were not prepared like himself to meet it. Utterly shattered in constitution, he had just repaired to Scarborough for the recovery of his health when the outbreak of the Rebellion summoned him to his post in Scotland. Unfortunately he did not ask for exemption from duty on account of physical inability. His leading motive for thus rejoining was his deep concern for the defenceless state of the island and the disaffection shared in by many of his friends and relatives. He often pointed out that "a few rebels might have a fair chance of marching from Edinburgh to London uncontrolled, and throw the whole kingdom into an astonishment." As we have seen, he was found by Cope in August to be so "extremely ill" that he could not be taken on the northern expedition. He remained at Stirling, where his wife, Lady Frances Erskine, a daughter of the Earl of Buchan, resided with some of her family.

The approach of the rebels from Perth was known. Gardiner wrote, "They are advancing to cross the Firth," and while he expressed his trust in Providence, he yet appears to have had none in the strong right arms of his own stalwart men.[1] Nothing was done by him to impede or to observe the movements of the enemy; yet for eight days and nights before their actual crossing he allowed his men to be harassed and fatigued by false alarms and consequent marching. On the 16th, after three more days of further exhausting and demoralising treatment, the legs of many of his soldiers were so swelled that they were obliged to "cut their boots off," and their courage and sense of military honour were artificially extinguished. A friendly historian states that the "judicious Gardiner frequently declared that had

[1] Doddridge, p. 141 *et seq.;* Cope's Trial, p. 75.

'Hamilton's dragoons been with him at Stirling, he could have stopped the enemy's passage.'" For their absence General Guest was locally responsible; but King George had returned to London on the 31st of August, and had then assumed direct control of all the troops in Britain. Although it is evident from the letter from Lord Tweeddale, already referred to, which Cope had received at Aberdeen, that the services of both regiments of dragoons would have been utilised for work against the rebels between Edinburgh and Stirling, no specific orders had been issued. With only his own regiment, somewhat above 350 in number, no one anticipated that Colonel Gardiner would have been able to stop the invading force; but, on the other hand, friend and foe alike expected that by hovering near the rebels, by at least threatening attacks on their weak and lengthened column of march, by cutting off their foraging-parties, and by harassing them in various ways, he would have caused constant trouble in the Highland ranks, and thus checked the quickness of their approach. It must be borne in mind that the rebels were wholly destitute of cavalry, and were only partially armed with short-range muskets, many of which were of an old pattern.[1] Gardiner, however, retreated before

[1] Henderson's Hist., pp. 40, 42.

they had actually crossed the Forth, and always "kept about six miles" in their front. It may, however, be remarked that the dragoons of that period were not specially trained for the duties of light cavalry.

On the 14th of September Prince Charles, after refreshing himself at Leckie House, advanced towards Edinburgh.[1] To quote the clear narrative of Lord George Murray: "We passed by Stirling, and the royal standard was saluted by some cannon shot from the castle. I sent into the town; they opened their gates, and sent bread, beer, cheese, and other provisions near to Bannockburn, where we halted. We lay upon a field east of Falkirk that night." Why the despatch of these much-needed provisions was permitted by General Blakeney, who commanded the castle dominating the town, is one of the military mysteries of the campaign.

It has been mentioned that on the 13th Colonel Gardiner had hastily retired to Falkirk, where he expressed to his old friend the Rev. Mr Adams, the minister of the town, his "most genuine contempt of life"; and his biographer states "that he seems for a while to have infused these sentiments into his men, for they expressed such a spirit in their march

---

[1] Lyon in Mourning, vol. i. p. 209; Jacobite Memoirs, p. 35.

from Stirling, that I am assured the Colonel was obliged to exert all his authority to prevent their making incursions into the rebel army, which lay very near him; and had it been thought proper to send him the reinforcements he requested, none can say what the consequences might have been; but he was ordered to march as fast as possible to meet Sir John Cope's forces at Dunbar, which he did."[1] It is a comfort in this shameful story to know that the rank and file had still the feelings natural to British soldiers, and felt as yet their degradation in having no choice but to obey such orders. But there is no ground for believing that the commands emanated from any one except their own colonel. It is impossible that Dr Doddridge's ready and confident excuse can be accurate, as at that very time Cope was embarking with the intention of landing at Leith, and it was not until three days later that he unexpectedly landed at Dunbar, the dragoons having by that time rapidly retreated to Musselburgh, five miles on the east side of Edinburgh. Moreover, had such been Gardiner's orders, he would never have written from Falkirk for reinforcements to enable him to stand his ground. Gardiner's mind must have become as enfeebled as his body, otherwise he would

[1] Dr Doddridge's Life of Colonel Gardiner, p. 141.

have realised that the speed of his own backward movements would have prevented the junction of other troops, had their services been deemed available by General Guest. He retired to Linlithgow on the approach of the rebels to Falkirk.

Having arrived at Falkirk, the Prince repaired to Callander House, the mansion of the Earl of Kilmarnock, where he was entertained. The Earl had dined in the afternoon with the dragoons at Linlithgow, and, having left their camp at six in the evening, was able to inform Charles of their exact position, and of what the officers thought were their colonel's plans.[1] He reported that it had been decided by Gardiner to dispute the passage of Linlithgow next day. This incident on the Jacobite side almost matches the attempt of Murray of Auchtertyre to capture his neighbour and friend, the Duke of Perth, by taking advantage of dinner hospitalities. The Prince resolved to forestall Gardiner's supposed plans by sending "a detachment to attack" his regiment. Lord George Murray states: "A thousand men went about one in the morning, which I commanded. There was not a hush to be heard the whole way, and I was much satisfied to find the men could march

---

[1] Lockhart Papers, p. 445; Jacobite Memoirs, p. 35; Murray of Broughton, p. 16.

in such order; and upon any emergency were perfectly obedient, though, when no enemy was near, they were not regular. When we came to the place, by four in the morning, we found the dragoons had gone off the night before; the rest of the army came to us at Linlithgow about ten, and we all marched three miles farther. Next night we got within three miles of Edinburgh, and took possession of the town by break of day, the 17th September." Such is Lord George's succinct narrative; but it appears necessary to add further particulars of some of the occurrences which led to that important event.

Gardiner was right in avoiding a night attack from superior infantry force; but ordinary military precautions would have prevented a surprise, and there was no need to hurry off in the darkness of the night, so as to bring ridicule upon his soldiers and to inspire their minds with the dread of a foe whom they were not permitted even to behold. On reaching Linlithgow the Highlanders had expected "a fine plunder." They found, however, only "the sacking frocks which the troopers used in dressing their horses," and they, according to the metrical historian of the Rebellion, Dugald Graham, raged because

"the sojers they had chaced
Left but their auld sarks in their haste."

It was on the 15th that an occurrence took place which marks at once the power of a chief over his clan and the looseness of the military bonds which held together the forces of the Prince. Not far from their bivouac stood Newliston, the mansion of Lord Stair, whose father had signed the paper which caused the massacre of Glencoe, and whose own name was attached to the recent proclamation offering £30,000 for the Prince's life. The grandson of the chief who with many of his relatives had, fifty years before, been so foully murdered, now commanded their descendants under Charles. It was apprehended that some mischief might be done to the property of the Earl, and a special guard was ordered to prevent any such outbreak of revenge, which would have seriously injured the Stuart cause. When, to use the words of Scott, Glencoe heard of this, he "demanded an audience of the Prince. 'It is right,' he said, 'that a guard should be placed on the house of Newliston; but that guard must be furnished by the Macdonalds of Glencoe. If they are not worthy of this trust, they cannot be fit to bear arms in your Royal Highness's cause, and I must withdraw them from your standard.' The claim was admitted, and not the smallest article in the house was destroyed, or even disarranged."[1]

[1] Tales of a Grandfather, vol. iii. p. 334.

The Highlanders were not permitted to enter Linlithgow, which had been so long a seat of Scottish royalty.[1] They lay quietly during the day on the banks of a rivulet a little to the east of its boundary. Charles himself was conducted to the palace and duly feasted. The provost happened to be a keen Jacobite, but he discreetly retired to Edinburgh, leaving his wife and daughters to wait upon the Prince "with tartan gowns and white cockades." In the afternoon the whole force moved forward to ground near the twelfth milestone from Edinburgh, and there bivouacked,—"all the officers, from Lord George Murray downwards, sleeping without any covering except their plaids." The Young Chevalier himself rested in a small farmhouse in the rear of the army. The last march to the capital was made with due caution, as attacks from the united regiments of cavalry were naturally anticipated. Murray of Broughton states that, "how soon all was ready in the morning the Chevalier drew up his army, six in front, making them close their files as much as possible, the country not allowing him to march in two columns, and advanced in the greatest order, not a man offering to quit his ranks, being ready to receive the dragoons, in case they should venture to attack them." At Todshall

[1] Chambers's Hist., p. 84; Blaikie's Itinerary, &c., p. 12.

he halted for two hours, and sent on reconnoitring parties. This slow advance, Home remarks, had the effect "of giving time for the terror of their approach to operate on the minds of unwarlike citizens in a divided city."

It has been shown that early in July Sir John Cope had been almost alone in realising the serious nature of the coming struggle, and had in vain entreated the Regency to take adequate precautionary measures. Under the astute direction of Murray of Broughton, the Jacobite party had worked so as to cause as little alarm as possible, and for that purpose had in general conversation and society minimised the strength and numbers of those who favoured a change of dynasty. In spreading this false sense of security they were aided by the Regency, who did their utmost to lull all visible cause of apprehension, and by many of the Whig party, who, headed by the Lord President himself, overrated the prudence, if not the loyalty, of some who afterwards supported the revolt. To speak otherwise than with confidence in the sagacity and vigour of Government was deemed treason. Cope's personal energy had been laughed at as needless "fussiness." In Edinburgh, the Jacobite party, more active than their opponents, had taken advantage of various and real causes of discontent, and though in numerical inferiority, had in the municipal elections five years before captured for their partisans the provostship and most of the magistracies. This gave them extensive authority, for at that time, besides large civic powers, the Provost had the control over the king's ships in the Firth of Forth, and was "sole military governor in the city."[1] The period of their tenure of office was just coming to a close, and a supreme effort was being made to oust them by the Whig party, headed by Mr George Drummond, a gentleman of high character, who had fought in the previous rebellion at the battle of Sheriffmuir and had already served as provost. It was most unfortunate that the elections came on exactly at the present crisis, but there is no just cause for the ridicule which has been poured upon the efforts of the rival parties. Both were influenced to a certain extent by motives of the highest national importance, and not by mere petty ambition to grasp at municipal dignities.

[1] Home's Hist., vol. iii. p. 36; Stewart's First Trial, p. 13.

CHAPTER V.

THE situation of Edinburgh favoured a successful resistance, as long as provisions lasted, against an irregular force who dreaded artillery, of which they themselves were destitute. Their inefficiency in attacking stone defence had only three weeks before been proved by their miserable attempt to capture the Ruthven Barrack with its garrison of a dozen soldiers, but commanded by one good sergeant. The north side of the city was secured by the North Loch at the foot of the lofty rock on which stands the castle. The cannon of that fortress swept the farther shore of the lake and the whole of the west and a portion of the southern fronts, while they could fire down the principal street of the city.[1] The part of the west side not occupied by the castle, and the whole

[1] It may be here noted for the benefit of those not intimately acquainted with the growth of the city of Edinburgh, that the North Bridge was not built till 1750, and that there were then no streets north of the North Loch, now the site of the Princes Street Gardens.

of the south and east sides, were surrounded by old walls from twelve to twenty feet in height and strengthened by bastions. The east side, in which the Nether Bow Port was situated, was that most easy of attack, as it was safe from the castle guns, and as houses beyond and higher than the walls had been there built. The usual garrison of old and invalid soldiers had been increased by Cope, who before leaving Stirling had thrown into it two companies of Lascelles's regiment. It had been further strengthened by the recent arrival of the artillerymen, who he had begged might be sent from London, principally for service with his own light guns.

For the defence of the town the magistrates still retained, in name and form, their ancient militia, called the trained bands, which consisted of sixteen companies with from 60 to 100 men in each.[1] The privates were enrolled and the officers appointed from the burghers of the city. 1400 stand of arms were always kept ready in the magazine for their use; but for many years these had been only used for show purposes on king's birthdays and like festivals. Disaffection to Government was, moreover, notoriously prevalent in their ranks. On account of the known existence of the same feeling, they had during

[1] Home's Hist., vol. iii. p. 56.

the Rebellion of 1715 been laid aside, and their arms had been intrusted to a body of volunteers. It was proposed to the Provost to follow a like course on the present occasion, but he refused, alleging his aversion to wound the feelings of any of his citizens.[1] Though the companies of the trained bands showed no unwillingness to parade when separately called out during the fortnight preceding the arrival of the Prince, no one had confidence in them as a body. Besides these there was the town guard, consisting of a company of foot, 126 in strength, better disciplined and armed.

When the real danger became apparent, the absence of preparation to meet it on the part of the Government or town authorities, and obvious inadequacy of these forces, caused the gravest anxiety to the supporters of the Hanoverian succession, and, as we have seen in an extract from a letter of Lord Milton's, a meeting of respectable inhabitants, holding loyal views, had been held on the 27th August to consider "what steps the community might legally take to frustrate the designs of his Majesty's enemies."[2] The idea of holding this meeting had a few days before been scoffed at with "insipid jests" by the Lord

[1] Stewart's First Trial.
[2] Home's Hist., vol. iii. p. 33; Stewart's First Trial, p. 32.

Provost. Its main propositions were "that the city should be forthwith put in a posture of defence, and that a body of 1000 men should be raised and armed." The Provost first objected on the ground that sufficient money could not be collected by subscription to pay the men, on which some citizens of known wealth and credit guaranteed funds for three months. He next objected on account of the illegality of the measure without the king's sanction, and in this he was supported by Lord Milton and the other Crown lawyers. Application for his Majesty's warrant was therefore necessary, but the desired permission did not arrive till the 9th of September. Meanwhile the news reached the city that Cope had marched to Inverness, thereby leaving the road to the Lowlands open to the Highlanders. The anxiety already felt at once ripened into genuine alarm and forced on further action. A contemporary journal narrates that on the 2nd and 5th September "some twenty gentlemen of known affection to his Majesty met,"[1] and, notwithstanding previous rebuffs, urged the Provost to give the necessary orders for repairs of the walls and for the adoption of other sensible and obvious precautions. He at length deigned to walk over a part of the walls with some of the gentlemen, including

[1] Stewart's First Trial, p. 35 *et seq.*; Professor Maclaurin.

Professor Maclaurin, whom he had asked to make out a plan for strengthening the defences, declaring at the same time that "he could not see but if 2000 men had a mind to get into the town they must succeed." It was not, however, till the 7th that orders were passed on the subject, and the Professor was constituted chief engineer. This duty could not have been laid on one more competent to perform it well. He was respected by all classes. His brilliant lectures, running over many years, had made mathematics a fashionable study, and he had trained in science the great majority of the military engineers then in the British service.[1]

About the same time a petition was placed in the Provost's hands, signed by many citizens, praying that they might be allowed to associate as volunteers, naming their own officers, and that General Guest should be asked to furnish them with arms from the king's magazine. His lordship deemed it an insult that such a paper should have been drawn up without his knowledge, and declared the request to be both unreasonable and treasonable.[2] On appeal, however, to the same high legal authorities who had decided against the

---

[1] Carlyle's Autobiography, p. 32.
[2] Home's Hist., vol. iii. p. 35; Stewart's First Trial, pp. 66, 101 *et seq.*; and Stewart's Second Trial, pp. 11, 42.

raising of a paid regiment without the royal warrant, these dignitaries now held that the proposal to raise volunteers was right and lawful. The Provost was, with some apparent reason, unable to perceive the exact distinction between the two classes of combatants, rendering the king's warrant necessary for the one and not for the other; but he felt it prudent to give way and permit the enrolment of volunteers, "insisting, however, on the privileges of his office" by the retention of the colonelcy for himself and of his right to name the officers. On the 11th, after a delay of five or six days, six captains were nominated by his lordship, each of whom was allowed to select two lieutenants, and the ranks were soon filled up by 4000 volunteers, "mostly substantial burgesses." But their unity and efficiency as a corps were ruined by the Provost's abstaining from appointing field officers, which caused each of the companies to be a little force independent of the others.[1]

On the 9th the king's sign-manual arrived for the enlistment of a regiment of 1000 foot. Again the Provost secured for himself the colonelcy and the selection of officers. Ample funds were soon collected. The sixteen ministers of the town alone, out of their moderate stipends, subscribed for the pay of 100 men,

[1] Culloden Papers, p. 262; Stewart's First Trial, p. 48.

and Maclaurin himself signed for a dozen. Circumstances, however, prevented recruits coming forward with the desired rapidity, and by the 15th there were not more than 200 men fit to march under arms.[1] Unhappily on the 10th the first series of the municipal elections began, and trades were so engaged in a variety of keen contests that both recruiting and work on the town ramparts were seriously impeded. With regard to the latter, Professor Maclaurin wrote to President Forbes thus: "I laboured night and day under infinite discouragements from superior powers. When I was promised hundreds of workmen I could only get as many dozens: this was daily complained of; redress was promised; but till the last few days no redress was made, and then it was too late." By the 16th, however, the embrasures had been cleared, and some eighteen cannon, procured from ships in Leith Roads, had been mounted on wooden platforms on the walls, so as to command the weakest places. Three of these raked St Mary's Wynd, and others flanked the curtains and gates.[2] Skilled men to work them were of course needed. General Guest would not spare one from the castle. His scruples were made known to the Provost, who was requested to procure out of his Majesty's ships in the Forth forty

[1] Culloden Papers, p. 262.   [2] Stewart's First Trial, p. 48.

or fifty sailors, experts in managing cannon. His lordship is recorded to have exclaimed, " By God! sir, while I am Provost of Edinburgh sailors shall not be admitted."[1] When pressed for his reason for this awkward and untimely decision, he answered " with some heat " : " My reason is plain, sir. If they should be admitted here, it would be, ' Damn your eyes ! Jack ; fire away and be damned !' and so they would fire upon and murder the inhabitants. It is my duty to protect the lives of the inhabitants, as well as to defend the town against the rebels." For this cause, both moral and humane, the cannon, procured and mounted with such difficulty, would have been rendered useless had resistance been attempted, and had the rebels ventured an assault. Ultimately there was one solitary sailor, "who was said to have skill in loading artillery," obtained from Leith to deal with all the guns![2] General Guest and the Provost were equally cautious as to their loading. The former objected to this very necessary process being performed by the royal artillery without a written order from the latter, which was positively refused. The intercession, however, of Professor Maclaurin and Mr Drummond induced the Provost to give a verbal order, with which, along with a written order from Mr Drummond, Lieutenant Bryden, the executive

[1] Stewart's Second Trial, p. 45.   [2] Ibid., pp. 121-193.

artillery officer, was very sensibly satisfied. The loading commenced on the evening of Sunday the 15th, and was not half over when, before eleven at night, the gunners were recalled to the castle. The Professor, however, undauntedly stuck to the work, but did not fully accomplish it till Monday afternoon.[1] By this time the gates had been barricaded, and the walls and other defences had been repaired, and, to use the words of the gallant old Professor in writing to Lord President Forbes, "the town was in a condition to have stood out for two or three days against men unprovided with artillery, unskilful, and then ill armed; and there was a double expectation of relief—viz., from the Dutch, and from Sir John Cope."

Colonel Gardiner, after his hurried retreat from Linlithgow on the night of Saturday the 14th, halted at Corstorphine, about three miles west of Edinburgh. He had not left behind any detachment or scouts of the enemy. Imagining that they were close at his heels, he kept his men under arms all the remainder of the night, in readiness, it may be presumed, for further flight. From his camp there came into Edinburgh very exaggerated accounts of the strength and proximity of the foe, not one of whom the soldiers had been permitted to come within sight of.

[1] Culloden Papers, p. 261.

These disturbing reports caused General Guest to summon early on Saturday to his house in Edinburgh a meeting of council, attended by the Crown officers and others, for the purpose of deciding what was to be done at this crisis. It was proposed that Hamilton's dragoons should be ordered from Leith Links to join Gardiner's at Corstorphine, and there offer battle to the rebels.[1] But the General objected on the ground that there was "no body of foot to act with the cavalry and draw off the enemy's fire." His own opinion was that Gardiner should retire, and join Hamilton's men on Leith Links. One of those present was Mr Drummond, who had just returned from London, and who had been named captain of the first College Company of Volunteers. He asked the General if 250 volunteers and 50 of the town guard would satisfy the need as a support to the cavalry, and was informed that these numbers would suffice. Mr Drummond at once repaired to the College Yards, where the volunteers, after only three days of preliminary instruction, were being taught for the first time how to load their muskets. He addressed to his own company a patriotic speech, which he ended, according to one of his most enthusiastic young pri-

---

[1] Stewart's First Trial, p. 109; Second Trial, p. 192 *et seq*. Home's Hist., vol. ii. p. 47. Carlyle's Autobiography, p. 111.

vates, Home the historian, by saying, "Now, gentlemen, you have heard the General's opinion, judge for yourselves: if you are willing to risk your lives for the defence of the capital of Scotland, and the honour of your country, I am ready to lead you to the field." Home continues, "That instant, the volunteers upon whom he had fixed his eye while he spoke threw up their hats in the air, and began a huzza, in which the company joined, and embraced the proposal." Mr Drummond then went from company to company, making similar stirring appeals to each. But he explained that "the resolution to conquer or die" on the field "was not proper for every person who had taken arms merely to defend the city; that it was suitable to young men not connected with families, and at liberty to dispose of their own lives." "Most of the volunteers in every company had no mind to march out of town, and some murmured at the proposal." Mr Drummond, however, mistook the loudness of the cheering for a general assent, and despatched a messenger to acquaint General Guest that the volunteers were ready to march out and engage the rebels. The General then sent a gentleman to request Provost Stewart to order fifty men of the town guard to join the volunteers. The Provost, their colonel, was very naturally displeased on receiving this message, as he had heard nothing previously about the scheme; but, after a little hesitation, he ordered the whole of the town guard and as many men of the Edinburgh regiment as were fit for duty to join the dragoons. On this, marching orders were sent to the regiment on Leith Links, and shortly after the horsemen dashed through Edinburgh, cheering and clashing their swords as they passed the volunteers, who had meanwhile assembled in the Lawnmarket. To this rendezvous they had been summoned by the sounding of the fire-bell, an unfortunate signal. Service was at the time being held in all the churches, which were wellnigh emptied when the dreaded sound was heard; and then, according to Home, "a universal consternation seized the minds of the people of every rank, age, sex, and party. The relations of the volunteers crowded about them, and mixed with their ranks. The men reasoned, and endeavoured to dissuade their friends; the women expostulated, complained, and, weeping, embraced their sons and brothers." Home proudly goes on to narrate that "neither the arguments of the men nor the tears of the women had any effect upon those volunteers" (of whom he himself was one) "who had agreed to Mr Drummond's proposal." But another ordeal lay before them. Home's company headed the volunteers, who were to follow the cavalry down the

West Bow to the Grassmarket, with the intention of marching through the West Port. It was, however, discovered that they had been followed by none of the other companies. A halt being made, it was ascertained that, while the men in the first company, who were unwilling to leave the city, had been kept apart during the halt in the Lawnmarket, the same precaution had not been taken with the others. Confusion had consequently occurred when the order to march was given to the whole. In a short time Sir George Preston of Valleyfield, one of the volunteer captains, brought down 141 more men who desired to take the field. These, with 42 of Drummond's own company, made up a detachment of 183 men—a number considerably short of the 250 promised to the General. While waiting to see if more were coming, the church services were concluded, and the clergy appeared on the scene. Dr Wishart, the respected Principal of the College and a leader among the loyal citizens, at once addressed the volunteers. He conjured them to remain within the walls which they had undertaken to defend. This, he said, they could do with effect, while their want of training and scanty numbers would make them useless on the field. During the long halt other similar speeches were made. On the other hand, Carlyle informs us, "The brewers brought out bread and cheese, and strong ale and brandy, in the belief that we needed it in marching on such an enterprise." Notwithstanding these bodily stimulants, it was evident that the clerical addresses had changed the resolution of many. Accordingly, after communication with the Provost and with his full approval, the volunteers were marched back to the College Yards, and dismissed until the hour appointed for settling the night guards who were to be posted round the whole city. The town guard and the detachment of the Edinburgh regiment had meanwhile marched to Corstorphine; but as no enemy appeared, they returned to join in the city night duties, though in a fatigued condition. Sir Walter Scott, among many other mistakes, attributes to General Guest the planning of this enterprise, and has not a word against its folly.[1] The opportunity for stopping, or at least impeding, the Highlanders on their long line of march from the Ford of Frew had been lost. Cavalry is essentially an offensive arm of the service. It was futile for them to take up a defensive position at Corstorphine, where they could only remain for a few hours, and where they might either be attacked or not, according to the option of an intelligent enemy. It is almost needless to say that the 300 untrained men, whose

[1] Tales of a Grandfather, vol. ii. p. 304, ed. 1830.

services the aged General bargained for, would have been practically powerless against masses of clansmen who knew how to march and use what arms they possessed. Sir Walter covers the volunteers with ridicule, as being the cause of the fiasco; but in fact they were the victims of the incapacity of others, and they did nothing of which brave men need have been ashamed. The Provost neatly utilised the occasion by adding a useful contribution to the spoils destined within two days to fall into the hands of the Prince. On receiving the order to take the field, Mr Dalyell, senior captain of the town guard, reminded his lordship of the bad condition of the arms of his men, on which he was authorised to help himself from those issued for the use of the incomplete new Edinburgh regiment, of which the Provost himself was colonel. The muskets were of the newly introduced pattern, being supplied with bayonets which fitted round their muzzles and rendered them capable of being fired with "fixed" bayonets. With the old pattern it was necessary to remove the bayonets on each occasion of loading the guns.

To add to the embarrassments of Provost Stewart on this busy Sunday, he was pestered by the arrival from outlying localities of small bodies of volunteers, who had ventured to dare the law and assemble to offer their services in defending the town. From the west Bruce of Kennet came in with 180 men, a gallant Dr Tait headed 50 from Dalkeith, and Sir Robert Dickson of Carberry led in 150 from his own neighbourhood of Inveresk. Small though these numbers were, they are sufficient to show that, had it not been for the crushing distrust of the king, there would have been no difficulty in obtaining the active support of the Lowlanders, who keenly felt the humiliation of not being permitted to strike a blow for what they thought the cause of religion and freedom. These little bands were received by the Provost with scant courtesy. He told the Dalkeith party that he had no arms to give them, and after they had obtained weapons from the castle, through the intervention of Lord Advocate Craigie, he declined to give them any orders. By the aid of the ever active Mr Drummond they were at length assigned quarters in the High School, and were posted for the night to defend an important part of the walls near the Cowgate Port. "They were not, however, supplied with meat, coal, or candle."[1] Sir Robert Dickson's men, who arrived later, obtained refreshments and shelter in "the New Church Isle"; but, in spite of many promises, did not succeed in being either armed or employed, and before the

[1] Stewart's Second Trial, p. 77.

following evening most of them had in utter disgust returned to their homes. The adventures of Bruce's men are not chronicled in the Stewart Trial, but there is no reason to believe they were more pleasantly dealt with.

On that Sunday evening there arrived in Edinburgh Brigadier-General Fowke, who had, in tardy compliance with Cope's entreaties for more officers, been sent by Government to assume command of the two cavalry regiments. He repaired at once to the house of the Lord Justice-Clerk, Lord Milton, where another council of "the king's servants," General Guest and "several other persons of distinction," were discussing measures of defence "should the rebels advance to attack the town."[1] Guest, Fowke, and others proposed to bring in a party of Gardiner's dragoons with a view "to suppress disorderly people, and to encourage those who were in arms for the Government." The Provost objected strongly to the plan; and finally it was agreed that the cavalry should continue posted at Coltbridge, about a mile west of Edinburgh. It seemed to be known to the meeting that Colonel Gardiner would fall back to that position as soon as darkness rendered his retirement invisible. This third movement, though otherwise advisable, must have

[1] Cope's Trial, p. 70; Stewart's Second Trial, p. 24.

given another depressing blow to his already dispirited men.

On Sunday evening there were available for the defence of the city upwards of 1100 armed men besides the town guard.[1] They were posted under the advice of Captain James Murray, Receiver-General of Customs, who on Saturday night had been tardily summoned, at Mr Drummond's suggestion, for the purpose of giving his experienced aid in military matters. The ramparts during the night were therefore fully manned by willing defenders, whose physical strength was, however, being worn out by watching for a foe who, as the Jacobite partisans must have known, were reposing placidly thirteen miles away. Carlyle and Home, afterwards well-known men and authors, were volunteer privates on the same guard. The following quotation from the former's Autobiography is interesting: "We had nothing to do all night but make responses every half hour, as the 'All's well' came round from the other guards that were posted at certain distances, so that a stranger who was approaching the city would have thought it was going to be gallantly defended. But we knew the contrary; for, as Provost Stewart and all his friends had been against any preparation for defence, when they yielded to the

[1] Stewart's Second Trial, p. 15; Carlyle's Autobiography, p. 121.

zeal of their opponents, they hung a dead weight on every measure. This we were all sensible of, and had no doubt that they wished the city to fall into the Pretender's hands, however carefully they might hide their intentions. At one o'clock the Lord Provost and his guard visited all the posts, and found us at Trinity Hospital very alert. When he was gone, 'Did you not see,' said John Home to me, 'how pale the traitor looked when he found us so vigilant?' 'No,' I replied; 'I thought he looked and behaved perfectly well, and it was with the light of the lantern that made him appear pale.' When relieved in the morning, I went to my lodging, and tried to get a few hours' sleep; but though the house was down a close, the noise was so great, and my spirits so agitated, that I got none." The Provost himself says that "at twelve at night he began the grand round, which lasted till four in the morning," and that "having gone home for an hour or two," he was on the streets again at six in the morning.[1] For having concentrated on himself the performance of more duties — military, civil, and political—than one man could possibly accomplish, the Provost certainly paid the penalty of having no rest at this period; but, on the other hand, he was rewarded by knowing every detail that was done or left undone,

[1] Stewart's First Trial, p. 113.

and by keeping the practical direction of the whole game in his own head and hands.

By four o'clock on the morning of Monday the 16th Captain Singleton, Fowke's major of brigade, was sent to him, requesting the services of the town guard and city regiment to support the cavalry in their new position at Coltbridge.[1] The fatigued men were as soon as possible despatched on this duty, and the Brigadier himself, attended by Lords Napier and Home, old Sir John Clerk of Penicuik, and many other gentlemen, shortly afterwards followed. Although an ample advance-guard of an officer and thirty men had been left at Corstorphine, and the camp had doubtless its own vedettes and sentries, the poor men had been kept under arms all night,[2] and presented a sorry sight to the reviewing general, who states : " I found many of the horses' backs not fit to receive their riders ; many of the men's and some of the officers' legs so swelled that they could not wear boots ; and those who were really to be depended upon, in a manner overcome for want of sleep."[3] Henderson, a historian friendly to Colonel Gardiner and a witness to the scene, thus describes that officer : " He was muffled up in a wide

---

[1] Cope's Trial, p. 74 *et seq.;* Stewart's First Trial, p. 114.
[2] Stewart's Second Trial, p. 188.
[3] Cope's Trial, p. 70 *et seq.;* Henderson's Hist., p. 43.

blue coat, with a handkerchief below his hat, and tied under his chin." Sir Walter Scott, another historian most friendly to Gardiner, remarks that "the retrograde movements from Stirling had had a visible effect on the spirits of the soldiers";[1] and Sir John Clerk, with even more truthful candour, says that the dragoons, from their retirements and frequent removals "for greater safety to themselves, were chiefly intimidated and *taught*, as I think, to be notorious cowards, for the Highlanders were naturally afraid of horse, and they" (the dragoons) "were sufficient to have put them all to flight; but our military councils were at that time infatuated." Although so near Edinburgh, the Brigadier found that the commissariat arrangements were as deficient as other details. Captain Singleton, about an hour after the review, was therefore "ordered to go to the castle to General Guest, and to acquaint him that both men and horses were in great want of *everything*"; and to request "that he would be pleased to give directions for somebody to wait on the Lord Provost to have them supplied." Singleton was also directed to state that the Brigadier was desirous of obtaining the General's permission to advance from the position on the Water of Leith at Coltbridge, and to attack the rebels, if they advanced; and if, after rest

---

[1] Tales of a Grandfather, vol. ii. p. 302.

and refreshments, "the dragoons were in a condition to do it to the purpose." A bold forward movement of this nature would have been effective in many ways. Hamilton's regiment could not as yet have been deeply infected with the personal-safety spirit which had been instilled into the other men, and would, well led, have shown the wonted courage of British cavalry, and their example would have brought heart back into Gardiner's horsemen. We are told that the Prince at this time was in a desponding mood, and a rapid march of the cavalry round a portion of his long marching column, and their breaking through it here and there, would have kept up the Highland respect for a mounted foe.[1] Delay in their advance, a most important object, would certainly have been caused, and the arrangements which were allowed to go on so smoothly between the Jacobites within and without the city would have been —perhaps fatally—disconcerted. General Guest, however, refused to sanction any such advance. He moreover stated that as the ground on the Edinburgh side of Coltbridge was unsuited for cavalry movements, and as a continuance in that position would entail more night work, which the cavalry were unfit for, a retreat had better be made thence to some place " where they might be of more service in joining Sir John Cope

[1] Henderson's Hist., p. 44.

at his landing, which he had reason to expect every hour."

There was some delay in sending out the provisions and provender demanded for the dragoons, and while they were being supplied an occurrence took place which materially added to the excitement and alarm already prevalent in the city.[1] About ten o'clock a well-known Edinburgh Writer to the Signet, Mr Alves, came to the Provost, when sitting with another municipal dignitary, and, according to his lordship's account, narrated that on that morning "he happened on his way to town to ride near the rebels. The Duke of Perth knew him, and ordered him to come nearer; and upon hearing that he was going to Edinburgh said, "I understand the Provost and magistrates are making great preparations against us; but we are resolved to pay them a visit. If they will keep their arms in their possession, and allow us peaceably into the town, they will be civilly dealt with; if not, they must lay their account with '*military execution*'"; and turning to a young man he called the Prince, he asked him whether or not that was his pleasure? which the other seemed to assent to. The Provost contented himself with saying, "Mr Alves, this is a most extraordinary message, but they will find we are not to be intimidated with

[1] Stewart's First Trial, p. 114.

threats." He then consulted two friends, who "were of opinion that it was most proper to neglect the message, and to take no step that might publish to the inhabitants the threatening they had received." No such caution was, however, given to Mr Alves, and about an hour afterwards Mr Robert Dundas, the Solicitor-General, found him at the market-cross causing general consternation to the townsfolk by proclaiming the Prince's threats, and the fatal consequences which must follow any attempt at resistance. Dundas at once conveyed the herald of alarm to Craigie, the Lord Advocate, who, after hearing Mr Alves's statement, in his own name and in the names of the Lord Justice-Clerk, and General Guest, who were both then with him, summoned to their presence the Lord Provost.[1] His lordship soon appeared, and was informed that in not arresting Mr Alves he had been tolerating treasonable practices, and that it was his duty at once to commit him to jail on a charge of high treason. A party of volunteers escorted him to prison. This action on the part of the Solicitor-General deserves special notice, as it is the sole recorded instance of personal energy in behalf of their royal master displayed at this crisis by any of the higher officials of the Crown — President Forbes always excepted. Had the opportunity on this

[1] Stewart's Second Trial, p. 23.

occasion been taken of arresting the Provost himself, as well as Mr Alves, the fall of the capital and much subsequent bloodshed and misery to Scotland might even then have been saved. But these "servants of the king" appear to have had no heart in acting against Prince Charles.

Captain Singleton with all speed carried the message of General Guest to Brigadier Fowke. The latter did not like it, and, seeing no necessity for retiring unless the enemy advanced in force, he directed a party of gentlemen, supported by some of the town guard, to ride out and reconnoitre the rebels.[1] During their absence Colonel Gardiner "very strongly and many times" represented to him the "bad condition of his regiment, in particular from its having been harassed and fatigued for eleven days and eleven nights, with little or no provision for the men or forage for the horses; and," he added, "if they stayed another night on that ground, it was to be feared his Majesty would lose two regiments of dragoons. But," he said, "the Brigadier might do as he pleased; for his part he had not long to live." All the field-officers were then called together, and unanimously agreed with Gardiner's opinion. About this time news came in that the rebels were really advancing in a body, and the Brigadier

---

[1] Cope's Trial, pp. 71, 75; Henderson's Hist., p. 44.

ordered the quartermasters to Leith Links to mark out the ground, and to provide forage for the horses and straw for the men to lie on. A little after 3 P.M. the gentlemen who had been reconnoitring brought intelligence that the enemy were not far from Corstorphine. They had met a similar party of gentlemen sent forward by the Prince for a like object. In riding back to Coltbridge they had been preceded by the advanced detachment of dragoons, who had retired, showing and spreading needless alarm. The Brigadier states that soon after " I marched off *slowly* towards Leith, with Colonel Gardiner and the dragoons." He sent back his brigade major and Adjutant Ker of Gardiner's regiment to direct the city troops to return to Edinburgh, and "to see that the rear squadron moved off in order and without hurry, as there were several defiles and stone walls" on their way. This way ran between the "lang dykes," then running along the ground now occupied by George Street, the highest portion of the New Town of Edinburgh. But the second part of the Brigadier's directions were not obeyed. The rear moved off with such unseemly haste that the retreat became popularly called the "Canter of Coltbrigg," and caused the citizens and others, unaware that the general movement had been ordered by General Guest, very naturally to attribute it solely to a panic throughout the whole body. This climax was near; but the occurrences of this day were merely the last lessons in the twelve days' training which led up to the sad end. Before the Links was reached Colonel Gardiner informed the Brigadier that the quartermasters had returned without being able to procure food and forage at Leith, and proposed that the march should be continued to Musselburgh, five miles farther to the east. This was done, and a short halt was there made.

Just as they arrived at Musselburgh they were joined by Lord Advocate Craigie. He had gone to the castle to see General Guest, with the object of persuading him to substitute a written for a verbal order directing a troop of dragoons to be sent into the city. The General, like others, anticipating a coming surrender, had before two o'clock abandoned his house in town and taken refuge in the castle, of which General Preston, his junior in rank but equal in years, held the command. When on the castle heights Craigie "observed," as he termed it in his evidence, "the dragoons marching eastward by the Long Dykes."[1] Having with difficulty obtained the written consent of the Provost to the admission of the troop, he resolved to ride

---

[1] Stewart's Second Trial, p. 26 *et seq.*

out to overtake the cavalry. On his way, near Abbeyhill, he met Mr Grosset, a commissioner of customs, and a zealous and gallant supporter of the Crown, who was proceeding on a mission to the Provost from Lord Justice-Clerk Milton, then "putting away papers" at Brunstane, his country house near Musselburgh. The message carried by Mr Grosset also urged the entry of horsemen into the town. The Lord Advocate should not have allowed him to proceed. As events were marching rapidly in Edinburgh, he should have contented himself with cancelling the written permission which he already had in his pocket. Simultaneously with Craigie's overtaking the dragoons, a despatch was brought to him from the Provost of Dunbar, acquainting him "that the fleet, on board of which Sir John Cope's troops were, was seen within the May Island about two o'clock; and that they would be at Leith with the next tide, which would happen in the night-time." Craigie says that "as he read his letter aloud, it was soon through the whole two regiments and to Brigadier Fowke." During the halt it was found that a bivouac at Musselburgh could not be conveniently made, and Colonel Gardiner offered to procure all that was necessary, in the shape of ground, provisions, and forage, near his own house of Bankton, which was situated four miles farther east, in close proximity to the almost united villages of Preston and Prestonpans. The Brigadier accepted the suggestion, and as the Colonel "was very ill and extremely weak," permitted him to seek much needed rest in his own home after making the necessary arrangements. Gardiner accordingly preceded the dragoons and carried out this arrangement. Fowke himself at Musselburgh went to the house of Mr Hugh Forbes, one of the principal clerks of the High Court, and there met the Lord Advocate and Dundas, the Solicitor-General, and was in communication with the Lord Justice-Clerk at Brunstane. While there, Mr Grosset returned from his mission to the Provost, whom he had found presiding over an excited meeting of his council and others in the Goldsmiths' Hall, and who had taken advantage of the opportunity of the Lord Justice-Clerk's having, as it were, reopened the question, by now declining to sanction the entry of any dragoons into Edinburgh. Mr Grosset was, however, again sent to his lordship with an official copy of the news of Cope's being off Dunbar, and of the probability of his arrival at Leith that night, together with a renewed offer of the services of the whole or any part of the two regiments. When at Mr Forbes's house the Brigadier wrote to Cope describing the local state of affairs, and mentioned what he had written to the Lord Advocate, who states that in the letter "he advised Sir John rather to land his troops at Prestonpans or North Berwick than at Leith, as he would be nearer the assistance of the dragoons, who were to be quartered that night at Prestonpans, or thereabouts." Fowke's local knowledge is not quite accurate, and probably he had no wish, from what he had that day seen of the discipline of his men, to take them back over the same ground without infantry support. After a halt for an hour and a half the regiments moved on to their intended bivouac. Out-guards and vedettes were duly posted. Just as they were settling down for one night's sound repose, one of their number, according to the local tradition, strayed a little beyond camp limits, and fell into a deep hole, whence the coal, which had there cropped up to within some few feet of the surface, had been extracted. He there in the dark made such a noise that the dragoons imagined that the Highlanders had got among them at last, and in wild excitement each man ran to saddle and bridle his charger. The dreadful news was sent to the officers, who had gone to sup at Lucky Vint's tavern, then a much-frequented hostelry in Prestonpans. The effect produced is narrated by Carlyle, who had, after delivering up his arms at the castle, left Edinburgh at half-past eight o'clock, and, accompanied by a younger and delicate brother, walked out slowly towards his father's manse at Prestonpans.[1] When he came to Lucky Vint's gate he said, "I was astonished to meet with the utmost alarm and confusion, the officers of the dragoons calling for their horses in the greatest hurry. On stepping into the court Lord Drummore, the judge, saw me. His house being near, he had come to sup with the officers. He hastily inquired 'whence I had come?' 'From Edinburgh direct.' 'Had the town surrendered?' 'No! but it was expected to fall into the hands of the rebels early to-morrow.' 'Were there any Highlanders on their march here?' 'Not a soul.' Lord Drummore turned to the officers and repeated the intelligence, and asserted that it must be a false alarm, as he could depend on me. But this had no effect, for they believed the Highlanders were at hand. It was in vain to tell them that the rebels had neither wings nor horses, nor were invisible. Away they went as fast as they could to their corps." Shortly afterwards the whole of the cavalry were heard making their way in the darkness by the narrow road at the back of the gardens, at the east end of Preston-

[1] Carlyle's Autobiography, p. 126; Home's Hist., vol. iii. p. 74.

pans, leading towards Dunbar and North Berwick. Pistols, swords, and other accoutrements, found strewn along the road in the morning, gave true tokens of the confusion of the panic flight.[1] Poor Gardiner had found in his house two of his daughters, Lady Frances, his wife, having been left in Stirling. He had retired to his room, after giving orders that he was not to be disturbed till four in the morning, his usual hour for rising; but, before the hurried start was made, Adjutant Ker was sent with six troopers "to fetch him off," and ride with his men. When the point on the main road was reached where a branch diverged to North Berwick, a portion of the dragoons went in that direction, thus adding some five miles to their ride. But the next forenoon the whole were reassembled at Dunbar, where Cope's force was beginning to land. Had a fair wind sprung up during the night and enabled the General to sail up the Firth, he would have found on his arrival at Leith that his cavalry were nearly thirty miles away.

[1] Carlyle's Autobiography, p. 127 ; Cope's Trial, p. 76.

CHAPTER VI.

It has been mentioned that on the eventful Monday, the 16th September, Prince Charles slowly approached Edinburgh. About two o'clock he drew up his forces to the west of Corstorphine, where, Murray of Broughton remarks, he was met by numbers of people from the city, "chiefly from curiosity." According to Henderson, he "was waiting with impatience the return of a letter which he, now quite morose and distrustful of the event, had sent by a trusty friend into Edinburgh." This information corresponds with the statement of Sir Walter Scott, that at this time the Prince's devoted adherent, Sir Robert Thriepland, brought to him the intelligence from his friends in the city which determined him to persevere in the attack. Charles must have been intensely relieved when he heard of the total retreat of his opponents, the dreaded cavalry, from the position on the Water of Leith at Coltbridge. This retreat removed from his sight a force which at any moment might have imperilled the existence of his army, and also rendered unnecessary a forward movement on his own part which might have brought his men under fire of the castle guns. He sent a summons to the Provost demanding the surrender of the town, and instead of advancing by the road now open up to the very gates of the capital, he turned to his right and bivouacked his troops near Gray's Mill, about two miles from Edinburgh, while he himself occupied the miller's house. He was here joined by Lord Elcho, the eldest son of the Earl of Wemyss, who five years before had with young Murray of Broughton paid his first court at Rome to the Old Chevalier.[1] Charles at once appointed Lord Elcho his first aide-de-camp, and at the same time warned him not to trust Lord George Murray (now so ably guiding the military portion of the enterprise), as he knew he had only joined to betray him.[2] The Prince then confided to him his distress for money, and joy-

---

[1] On this visit to Rome Lord Elcho had been placed back to back with the Prince, the two being of the same age and about the same height, to see which was the taller. The Old Chevalier then assured his youthful courtier that the loyalty of his father would be repaid with interest when he himself ascended the throne of Britain.

[2] Ewald's Life of Prince Charles, pp. 46, 113, 374, quoting from Lord Elcho's Journal.

fully accepted the loan of £1500, which Lord Elcho's younger brother, who had recently inherited the wealth of his maternal grandfather and was on the point of marrying a daughter of the Duke of Gordon, had presented to him as a token of sympathy with the cause when he heard of his intention of personally joining the Stuart standard.[1]

During this Monday the streets of Edinburgh were filled with excited citizens; and even before the retreat of the dragoons the Jacobite party were skilfully utilising the alarm, which Mr Alves's terrible message had much increased, by handing about petitions begging that "the magistrates would, before deciding on defending or giving up the town, call a meeting of the inhabitants, and consult them as to what was proper to be done." Hitherto the loyal

[1] Sir Walter Scott, in 'Tales of a Grandfather' (vol. ii. p. 328), diminishes this sum to £500, and styles it a "gift" from the Earl of Wemyss, and not an advance from the son. Its nature, however, is proved by the persistent, but vain, efforts of Lord Elcho in after years to recover the money when he had become an exiled and impoverished pensioner of the French king, and when it was quite within the power of Charles to have given repayment. The only and characteristic answer he could get to his applications was that the Prince had no intention of shirking his obligations, and that he would pay the sum—when he succeeded to the throne. Sir Walter also misled his readers and after-writers by apologetically stating that the Earl "was too old to take the field in person." Lord Wemyss was only forty-seven years of age, and needed no excuse for preferring his usual safe and pleasant life in Paris to risking his titles, estates, and head in a rash rebellion.

party had, as Captain James Murray remarks, "shown a good countenance"; but the news of the unexpected retirement of the regulars, whom all looked on as the backbone of the defensive force, changed the fears and anxiety of many into helpless anger and despair. The Provost alone was energetic. He stated in his defence at his trial that he "immediately caused the drum to go about, and order the inhabitants to retire from the streets" to their houses—a measure which only added to the uproar; and he conspicuously busied himself in shutting and "barricading" all the gates. He then returned to his council in the Goldsmiths' Hall amid the cries of the people, "What! would you have us all murdered by defending the town after the dragoons have run away?" The hall was packed by an audience, principally Jacobites, from whom the Provost demanded if they meant to enforce by numbers their demands for surrender. Knowing well how matters stood, he acted with plausible fairness and loyalty by sending three bailies to beg that the Lord Justice-Clerk, the Lord Advocate, and the Solicitor-General would come and assist them with their counsel, by which alone he pledged himself to be guided. Their absence from the town enabled him to publicly lament that "he found himself destitute of the advice he most relied on at this critical juncture."[1] Several military officers were sent for, but none had remained in town except Captain James Murray and Major Cochrane of the Excise.[2] The Provost had never concealed his private opinion that it would be wrong to defend the town; but now, specially addressing these gentlemen, he very warmly and officially declared his desire that the defence should not be abandoned. His first reason was that it would be a pity not to utilise the ramparts, in the repair of which so much town money had been expended; he then dwelt on "their having lately plighted their faith to his Majesty that they would do their utmost, stand for the support of his person and Government, and for the defence of the town";[3] and after stating that better terms might be hoped for, if they held out and at last surrendered with arms in their hands, he said that he himself "would do his duty, if he was to leave his bones upon the walls." Captain Murray was then asked if he thought the town was tenable, and replied that he pitied the

[1] Lord Milton had left in the forenoon, as has been said; but as he returned after dinner he met a crowd in the Canongate, who informed him that the rebels were already entering the city by the West Port. He believed the news which every one thought probable, and returned to Brunstane (Home's History, vol. iii. p. 58).

[2] Stewart's First Trial, pp. 86, 118; Second Trial, pp. 140, 47.

[3] Stewart's Second Trial, p. 174.

Provost, because he foresaw that the decision on this important question would chiefly lie upon him; that "they had hands enough; but that he and the other gentlemen present were the best judges of their hearts. If, however, they entertained any thoughts of delivering up the town, they were not to add to that reproach the crime of delivering the king's arms to the rebels."[1] It is further recorded that the captain then turned towards the principal clerk of the city and added with an oath, "If they do, some people may hang for it."[2] This was the second plain warning Provost Stewart had that day received that he was treading on the dangerous ground of treason. He avoided making any awkward promises by saying to the meeting, "I want, gentlemen, that ye should also give me your opinion — for it is by *your* opinion I am to conduct myself; and if you come to the resolution of defending the town, I will go wherever the danger is greatest, and defend it to the last."[3] No such resolution was come to. Towards the close of this meeting Mr Grosset appeared with Lord Milton's message regarding the entry into the city of dragoons, which gave the Provost, after a long wrangle, the chance of withdrawing the written sanction for this measure, wrung

---

[1] Stewart's Second Trial, p. 140. [2] Ibid., p. 174.
[3] Ibid., p. 183.

from him about two hours before by the Lord Advocate and Solicitor-General.

Many of the surrender party still pressing into the hall, and a noisy crowd of them thronging round the entrance, the Provost now adjourned the meeting to assemble at once in the larger building, called the "New Church Isle," which was soon filled almost entirely by Jacobites. It was all-important for the success of what was believed to be their policy to delay for a short time the final settlement of matters till the Prince was closer at hand, and quick communication with him could be established. When ordering the adjournment the Provost also directed the fire-bell to be rung. Even in ordinary times its sound invariably caused a general panic, as the houses in Edinburgh were high and inflammable, and no one at first knew where the danger had arisen. Its ringing served another purpose. It had unfortunately been ordered to be the signal for the volunteers to assemble at the Lawnmarket. Their patience and energies had been severely tried by having, after a night on the defences, been kept all day under arms, but without specific orders from their colonel, the Provost. Included in their ranks were the most active and zealous of the substantial burgesses, who supported the existing Government. Faithful to their military duty, and believing an attack to be imminent, they assembled at the rendezvous, and were consequently absent from the meeting which was about to decide the fate of the capital. The Provost states that on his way to the New Church Isle he did all he could to reanimate the concourse of people in the street, but while he was talking a gentleman rode up "with a message from Lieutenant-Colonel Whitney" (second in command of Gardiner's regiment) "desiring he would order the dragoons' baggage to be forthwith sent out to them, because they were going to Haddington, as they found they had been greatly deceived in the number of the rebels, for now they computed them to be near 8000. This account, given in the hearing of the crowd, did greatly contribute to increase the terror of the inhabitants, who were heard crying everywhere, 'What a madness it was to pretend to stand out against such a number.'" It is, however, also testified at Stewart's trial that he then remarked, "If the troops were retired, then *all* is over," a declaration which certainly was not of a reanimating tendency.

After quelling with difficulty the noise at the great meeting in the church, the Provost made another loyal speech, which, with true prophetic spirit, he foresaw might be of use at a future possible trial.

He complimented his audience "on the noble stand they had hitherto made for the defence of the city, and he hoped they would not now give it up: as for himself, he would be the first man to mount the walls in case of danger."[1] "Nevertheless," as one of his principal witnesses testified, "he did not observe that his words made any deep impression; for the generality of the audience continued to declare their sentiments against defending the town, and only a few spoke to the contrary." Prominent among these few were two ministers of the Church of Scotland. The first on the scene was the Rev. George Logan, who heard of the nature of the meeting when he was discussing affairs "with some others of his brethren, ministers, in the coffee-house." Principal Wishart shortly after made his way in, and found Mr Logan standing on a bench and strenuously opposing a proposition to send out representatives to treat with the rebels, which, he truly remarked, was inviting them into the town. Mr Logan and the Principal proposed instead that his Majesty's troops should be sent for. This was hooted by the audience, who raised cries of "No dragoons! they are gone! they are fled!" A proposition was made that the town should be delivered up, on which the Principal dared the

[1] Stewart's First Trial, p. 89; Second Trial, pp. 165, 189, 32, 35.

meeting, by stating that before making that proposal the Provost should have purged the place of the known enemies to Government. This was received with a general hoot, and one of the audience called out that the Principal himself was the first who should be expelled. "Great laughter," the reverend gentleman in his evidence good-naturedly states, followed this sally. Bailie Hamilton then pointed out to the Provost, who was sitting as President in the chair reserved for the use of the Moderator of the General Assembly of the Church, that he should at least give orders to the volunteers to deposit their arms in the castle to prevent the rebels getting them. No answer was vouchsafed to the suggestion. About this time Sir George Preston of Valleyfield, a nephew of the old governor of the castle, whose company of volunteers with Mr Nimmo's had all day been "planted" by the Provost's orders at the Netherbow, made his way into the meeting and demanded orders from his colonel. The reply was, "I cannot come yet; by-and-bye." On this Sir George exclaimed, "If you are proposing to deliver up the town, it is time that I should know what I am to do. I cannot stay." The Provost, thus pressed, directed him to march the companies to the alarm-post at the Lawnmarket. "Then"—to quote the evidence of the

Principal—"the Provost put the question, 'Who are for defending the town? if any, let them speak!' To which the deponent said, 'I am, though I be here alone.' Sir George and one or two more said the same; but the generality of the meeting were of a different opinion. The Provost then put the question, 'Shall we send any to treat with them?' On which the deponent said, 'I hoped never to have lived to hear such a question put by a Lord Provost of Edinburgh.' The deponent and Sir George left the meeting."

On Preston's reaching the Lawnmarket with the two companies from the Netherbow, he met parties of the other four companies returning unarmed from the castle after having handed in their arms. He states that he thought it was high time to follow their example. The other companies had assembled at the alarm-post on the sounding of the fire-bell. Their captains were summoned to the meeting, and were very long in returning. Intelligence, however, in various ways reached the ranks as to the nature of the resolutions which were being passed. Dusk was approaching, and the impression became universal that a capitulation was about to take place, and that "they with arms in their hands were to be put into the hands of the rebels." At length the captains came back, and after consulting the other officers, Lieutenant Lindsay was sent to explain matters to General Guest, who, being senior in army rank, had just superseded General Preston in the command at the castle, and to ask his leave to hand in their arms. This was done without the knowledge of their colonel, the Provost. The lieutenant was told that the General knew all about the state of affairs already, and that he expected the arms without loss of time. Accordingly about sunset (6 P.M.) this measure was carried out, Mr Drummond leading with his No. 1 company. One of that company, Carlyle, states, " We were glad to deliver our arms lest they should have fallen into the hands of the enemy, though not a little ashamed and afflicted at our inglorious campaign." John Home, another volunteer, adds, " Many laid down their arms with visible reluctance, and some with tears."[1] On hearing what the Edinburgh men had done, those volunteers from the neighbourhood who had received arms likewise handed in their weapons. The Dalkeith contingent, determined not to be caught in a trap, obtained ladders, and descending the walls as soon as it was dark, returned to their homes. Scott and other writers have heaped ridicule on the pusillanimous conduct of these gallant men.

[1] Carlyle's Autobiography, p. 124; Henderson's Hist., vol. iii. p. 61.

But they did nothing worthy of reproach. They were not responsible for the unfortunate fiasco on the previous forenoon, and during their short military existence they acted like men of courage, good sense, and honour.

Sir George Preston was right in his remark that it was high time that his men, while they had it in their power, should place their arms in safe custody; for just as the arms were being deposited in the castle, a letter, claiming them for himself, was received at the great meeting by the Provost from a personage who styled himself "Charles, Prince Regent." Its coming was not in a very royal fashion. At Stewart's trial Donald Mackay, caddie, testified that the missive had been placed in his hands, as he was standing outside near the church, by a gentleman dressed in black, of whom he remembered the face but not the name, and who accosted him thus: "Here is a letter to the Provost—you must give it to him; and here is threepence for your pains, and next time I see you I'll give you a shilling." Donald dolefully added, that a day or two after he saw in Edinburgh the gentleman, "who was then an officer in the service of the rebels, and craved from him his shilling that he had promised him; but he did not get it." However that may be, the caddie, not being able himself to enter the New Church, gave it to a gentleman standing outside, who declared that he took it in and saw it put into the Provost's hand.[1] Scarcely had it been opened by one of the municipal officials, Deacon Walter Orrock, than it was perceived and at once became generally known that it bore the signature of "Charles, P.R." A great noise at once arose. Some shouted that it should be read, others that it should not. The Provost then proclaimed, "I cannot be witness to the reading of this letter," and, dismissing the meeting, he returned to the Goldsmiths' Hall, whither several of his council and many of the inhabitants followed him. There the controversy reopened with even greater fury. Some urged that the letter ought to be read; others called out that doing so would be treason. At length it was agreed that the town's legal advisers should decide the point. Two out of these three gentlemen were, however, found to have already fled from the doomed city, and when the document was glanced at by the third, Mr Solicitor Patrick Haldane, he at once withdrew, declining to give any opinion, and saying that these matters were too high for him. Upon this the Provost, in an agony of hesitation and fear, real or simulated, exclaimed, "Good God! I am deserted by

[1] Stewart's Second Trial, pp. 110, 113, 166; First Trial, p. 121.

my arms and by my assessors."[1] But after some more demur the letter was quietly read. It was written with the wonted tact of Murray of Broughton, and showed a full knowledge of city politics. The Provost and magistrates were summoned to admit the Prince Regent into "the capital of his Majesty's ancient kingdom of Scotland," and the document continued, "If you suffer any of the usurper's troops to enter the town, or any of the cannon, arms, or ammunition now in it, whether belonging to the public or to private persons, to be carried off, we shall take it as a breach of your duty, and a heinous offence against the king and us, and shall resent it accordingly." All protection was promised if admission was peaceably given; but it concluded by saying, "If any opposition be made to us, we cannot answer for the consequences, being firmly resolved at any rate to enter the city; and in that case, if any of the inhabitants are found in arms against us, they must not expect to be treated as prisoners of war." After these threats were read, according to Provost Stewart's statement, "nothing was to be heard but loud cries against a fruitless opposition, and against delivery up of the town's arms to the castle, which it was said would occasion destruction to the city." It was then

[1] Stewart's First Trial, pp. 113, 121, 166; Second Trial, p. 56.

agreed that a deputation of four bailies should forthwith be sent out to the Prince "to beg that hostilities might not be commenced against the city until they had time to deliberate." The embassy passed through the West Port on their mission between seven and eight o'clock.

But troubles were thickening over the Provost's head. On the volunteers depositing their arms, staunch old General Preston at once ordered Ensign Robertson to start with a party of soldiers to bring up to the castle the cannon that were on the walls, or otherwise to render them useless by spiking them and knocking off the trunnions.[1] That officer was, however, soon followed by a messenger from General Guest (who, as has been said, had a few hours before superseded Preston in command) directing him not to proceed with the work without the concurrence of Provost Stewart. This forced the ensign to send first a sergeant and then a gunner to try to obtain that permission. But the Provost answered that "he had no authority to give, as his dragoons were gone eastward and his volunteers had laid down their arms." He gave them, however, the fullest leave to do with the cannon what they liked—"without his liberty." This reply, reasonable under the circumstances, was con-

[1] Stewart's Second Trial, pp. 99, 177, 188.

veyed to General Guest, who, refusing to allow the qualified permission to be acted upon, ordered the return of the party, saying that "the proper time was over for effectuating such work, as darkness had come on." The General added that "the Provost had lost the proper opportunity, and that the party might, if they remained any longer in the town, fall into the hands of some flying party of the enemy." Thus by the wilful inaction of the civil and military authorities compliance was given to the Prince's behest, as far as it concerned large guns.

The arms of the newly raised city regiment had a narrow escape from a similar fate. The Provost and his friends, afraid, as they declared, of the cruelty of the rebels on the one hand, and of their being possibly called to account at some future date by Government on the other, determined to give no orders whatever on the subject; but agreed "that the soldiers possest of those arms should be privately acquainted to return them to the castle." Had the individual privates been thus left to act for themselves, few would probably have cared to carry out the suggestion. Dean of Guild Allan, however, whose political sympathies do not seem to have been in accord with those of his chief, intervened, and sent an order to the adjutant of the regiment, Lieutenant Burns, to march the men up to the castle and give in their arms.¹ This was done after some demur on the part of the officer, who very properly hesitated to disarm the soldiers without the direct command of his colonel, the Provost.

The disposal of the arms of the trained bands caused more difficulty. There were 1250 muskets, besides 200 said to be "inefficient." An incident aided the Provost in deciding how to act. It has been mentioned that application had been made for the egress from the city of the baggage of the dragoons. After some delay the Netherbow gate, which had been closed at four o'clock, was opened for that purpose. Many townsfolk and others had been unexpectedly kept out, and as the portal opened they naturally crowded in. The mounted baggage escort drawn up inside imagined that these innocent citizens were ferocious Highlanders, "and rode off in great terror, as hard as they could, to the castle."² "Upon this alarm," says the Provost, "the commandant of the trained bands, Robert Tennent, put him in mind of the threatening sent to the town, that every man found in arms should be put to death, and asked what the trained bands at the Weigh-house and West Port should do when the rebels had already burst in at the other end of the town. The only

[1] Stewart's First Trial, p. 123; Second Trial, pp. 124, 114.
[2] Stewart's First Trial, p. 124; Second Trial, pp. 124, 126, 179, 197, 123.

answer any man alive could give was that they should quit their arms to avoid being massacred." These gentlemen must have had a strong private opinion that the alarm was false, as the rebels could not have marched all round the town without being seen. Nevertheless Captain Wemyss was sent to order the three companies of trained bands who were on duty to lay down their arms. He appears to have disliked his mission, for he only gave the order to the company at the Weigh-house, the captain of which refused to obey until he had sent his ensign to the Provost, and had ascertained the correctness of the order. The company was then dismissed, and the arms abandoned where they were. Shortly after the issue of the order, the Town Council being in the Council Chambers, grave discussion took place on the subject, and Dr Lauder, one of the members, was deputed to go to the castle for the purpose of explaining to the military authorities the awkward position in which the Council were placed, and of prevailing upon them to send down a party to bring up the city arms. Dr Lauder was selected for this mission because he happened to be a near relative of General Preston. Unfortunately, however, it was past eight o'clock before he reached the fortress, and by that time this very old veteran had gone to bed. He therefore had to interview the equally aged soldier, General Guest, whom he found very wide awake. The latter cut short all the doctor's explanations, and demanded, "Will your Provost give me a written order to send a party for the arms?" On being told that this was the very thing he dared not do, Guest flew into a passion and declared, "I will send no party unless he sends me a written order." Had the General been loyal to his king, a written order, or even no order at all, would have been immaterial to him, provided he saved the weapons from falling into the hands of the Prince. The nature of the decision was probably anticipated by the Provost; but the matter was not yet ended. The two companies of the trained bands at the West Port had not, as intended, received the command to quit their arms, and were seen at their post by the vigilant Bailie Mansfield, prepared to send a volley on any foe, when a second deputation left for the rebel camp at two on the Tuesday morning. The bailie hastened to inform the Provost and his friends of the mistake, which might have ruined their whole surrender scheme. The senior captain of the companies was sent for, chid for remaining so long at his post, and ordered at once to disarm and dismiss his men, leaving the weapons in the guard-room.

Scarcely had the deputation of bailies left the hall

between seven and eight o'clock on their mission to
Gray's Mill than Mr Grosset again appeared, having
been despatched in hot haste from Musselburgh by the
Lord Advocate with the original letters from Dunbar,
announcing that Cope's little fleet had been seen off
that town. Had the news arrived half an hour sooner
the fate of the capital might have been changed; but
now there was truth in the Provost's remark, after
reading the letters, "They are come too late, for the
Council had agreed to capitulate, and had sent some of
their number to treat about the terms." Grosset, however, begged that a messenger should be sent to recall
them, as they had proceeded on foot. The Provost
agreed, and Bailie Mansfield was selected for the duty.
His Jacobite tendencies are in evidence on Stewart's
trial, in which there is no mention of his being a swift
runner. Meanwhile ex-Provosts Drummond and Mac-
aulay came into the council chamber and demanded
that the alarm-bell should again be rung, that the
defence should be resumed, and the dragoons recalled.[1]
Grosset had authority from Brigadier Fowke to offer
the return of a part or the whole of the dragoons, but
he did not press that point, because he saw that all
faith in these horsemen had vanished. The Provost
answered, "That they must be tender of the blood of

[1] Cope's Trial, p. 76; Stewart's Second Trial, pp. 74, 170.

their fellow-burghers; that the rebels might hear the alarm-bell; and should those who had been sent out have arrived in camp, the rebels might hang them like rats." A keen discussion took place, and Grosset with ex-Provost Coutts was authorised to go to the castle and ask General Guest if he would sanction the re-issue of the arms which had been delivered up. The General's reply was that the Provost had still the city arms, which he might use at his discretion; and as to the other arms, if he *wrote* saying that there was a good spirit appearing among the people, and desired him to give up the arms, he might comply,—a qualified promise not likely to be put to the test. On their return to the council chamber a fierce debate was still going on, but ere long Mr Grosset was desired to inform the Lord Advocate that, "as the messenger" (Bailie Mansfield) "whom they had sent after their deputies had not overtaken them, the Council were come to a resolution not to defend the town." Mr Grosset then insisted on having this message in writing, on which the Provost declared that he had already put too much in writing that day, and he would write no more on the subject.

After the disarming and dispersion of the other defenders of the town, there only remained the city guard, consisting of 120 men. Most of them had been under arms and marching about all Sunday, and a third of them had been on duty on Sunday night.[1] They had been called out again at 4 A.M. on Monday morning, and many of them were tired out on their return from Coltbridge in the afternoon. But the whole were kept on duty till 8 P.M., when their senior captain, Dalyell, received orders from the Provost to keep on as the night guard of the town a third of the company, out of whom fourteen men were to be sent to the Netherbow Port, which the volunteers had, by order, left two hours before. Between three and four on Tuesday morning Captain Dalyell, while on duty at the guard-house, was informed that the whole of the Netherbow detachment "had got themselves drunk," and from the rest of his men he could only find six who were fit to replace them. In command of these six there was not even one non-commissioned officer. Fatigue and Jacobite hospitality may possibly be credited with the inefficient condition of the remainder. Dalyell knew well what was intended to be done. At five o'clock in the evening he had told the senior officer of the trained bands at the West Port that the town was to be delivered up. After despatching the six privates he, without being relieved, abandoned his post at the Court of Guard, and "went

---

[1] Stewart's Second Trial, pp. 145, 123, 149, 151.

to his own house." In his evidence he gives no reason for thus acting; but he naturally had no wish to stay and receive the expected visitors. The municipal "keeper of the Netherbow Port" was a citizen named James Tait, into whose custody the keys had been given after the exit of the dragoons' baggage, a little after 8 P.M. That functionary states that he was obliged to go to bed at "eleven o'clock, having been kept out of bed the two preceding nights with the volunteers, and that he committed the charge of the port to his servant James Gillespie." He adds that "he had received no orders about the manner of keeping the port, and that it was the ordinary custom to open the port as people called either going out or coming in." Gillespie testifies that Mr Tait "gave him orders, whatever chairs or coaches were entering the town or going out, to open the port and let them pass."

The deputation returned from the Prince's camp at about ten o'clock, bringing a written answer, signed by Murray of Broughton, who had conducted the parley with them. Charles refused to give other terms than those in the summons sent from Corstorphine, and demanded a positive answer before two in the morning.[1] He had asked what had become of the arms of the volunteers and Edinburgh regi-

[1] Home's Hist., vol. iii. p. 65; Henderson's Hist., p. 46.

ment, and being told that they were delivered into the castle, he said with great warmth, "If any of the town arms are missing, I know what to do." A similar warning was contained in the letter brought back by the deputies. Yet Murray in his recently published Narrative speaks slightingly of the importance of these arms transactions — his obvious motive being to shield his friend Provost Stewart, whom he elaborately vindicates from any disloyalty to the Hanoverian Government, and whom he styles "the only man in the city who exerted himself the most to bar the enemy's entry."[1] On their return to the city the deputation found the Provost, his Council, and some other citizens in their chamber, and they continued deliberating what was to be done till the clock struck the ominous hour of two. It was then agreed that a second deputation of five officials, headed by ex-Provost Coutts, should proceed to the Prince's camp for the ostensible purpose of craving a further delay of seven hours, in order that the magistracy might have still more time for consideration. With the knowledge that the value of a few hours was of even more importance to the Chevalier than it was to themselves, they could scarcely have hoped that this request could be granted; and the real object of

[1] Murray of Broughton's Hist., pp. 17, 18.

their mission, in all probability, was to arrange that a permitted and peaceable occupation, which might bring them into future trouble, should have the fictitious appearance of an unavoidable capture by force of arms. This double character exactly suited the wishes of the Prince also, as he thereby gained possession of the capital without the effusion of blood or destruction of property, and without incurring the possibly ruinous risks of either delay or an actual assault, while he was sure of popular glory from having apparently performed a bold military exploit. Accordingly, Lochiel and Colonel O'Sullivan with 1000 of the best disciplined Highlanders were despatched round the south side of the town, so as to reach the Netherbow Port on its eastern face shortly before daylight, between four and five o'clock. No scaling-ladders or other means of making a forced entry were taken; and Murray of Broughton's Narrative, which on this point may be relied on, makes it clear that no assault was contemplated. Were further proof of this needed, it lies in the fact that the diplomatist Murray was sent to guide the party and aid the commanders with his counsels and intimate local knowledge. Had fighting been anticipated, his warlike namesake, Lord George, would have been selected for the duty. Broughton says "that they had strickt orders to behave with all moderation to the inhabitants, and that the sogers should not be allowed to touch spirits, and to pay for whatever they got, promising them two shillings each so soon as they rendered themselves masters of the place." No shot from musket, swivel-gun, or cannon was fired at the party from the ramparts, along which, during the whole previous night, the call of "All is well" had passed from sentinel to sentinel; and no challenge was given even from the gateway battery as the Camerons formed up close to the port itself. The gates were not at once thrown open, and Murray, who had a strong regard for his own life, says that he " proposed to retire to a place called Saint Leonard's Hills, and after securing themselves from the cannon of the castle, to wait the Chevalier's orders." Before, however, a retreat was actually made, all anxiety was relieved. For just at this time from within the city there approached the gate a coach which had brought the second deputation from the Prince's camp. After leaving the embassy at Mrs Clark's tavern, where the Provost and his Council then were, it was proceeding to the stables in the Canongate. It was stopped by private Corsar, the senior of the six privates who shortly before had been sent to guard the Netherbow Port. According to that soldier's evidence, he refused to allow the coach to pass, although the driver declared that he had the permission of Provost Coutts; "upon which the under-keeper of the port, James Gillespie, came up, and, without having any discourse with either the coachman or postilion, said, 'I have an order to let out that coach.'" To this Corsar politely replied, "Oh, sir, it is well if you have an order to let it out; you have the keys of the port; you must answer for it, and I have nothing to say." "Then," he adds, "the port was opened, and the coach drove out, and was not past me two yards when the Highlanders rushed in, and Lochiel gripped me by the arm." That chieftain rapidly marched his men up to the Parliament Square and Court of Guard, whence he sent detachments to occupy the gates and walls. It has been mentioned that the captain on duty of the city guard had been left at his post. When his soldiers from the Netherbow told him of the invasion, he says that he sought out the Provost, and found him with others of the Council already "in company with a rebel officer, whom he afterwards knew to be Colonel O'Sullivan."[1] He then made his report of the capture of the city, which General Wightman, who was present, terms "a concocted surprise."

The historian Home, who was in Edinburgh at the

[1] Stewart's Second Trial, p. 147.

time, dwells on the quietness with which Lochiel was able to carry out all his important work, and adds,— "When the inhabitants of Edinburgh awaked in the morning, they found that the Highlanders were masters of the city."[1] There is ample proof that his record is on this matter true. Yet modern writers claim for the "tame surrender" the character of a noisy victory, gained by the bold strategy of the Prince. Sir Walter Scott, whose sequence of details and even words are to a great degree those of Murray of Broughton, adds to his narrative such warlike expressions as *coup de main*, "forlorn-hope," and "taken by storm."[2] Lord Mahon also twice uses the last term.[3] Chambers, too, on the sole authority of one anonymous Highland officer, states that the rebels rushed into the High Street "with battle outcries,"[4] elsewhere called "hideous yells"; and on information from an aged female, whose mother had been a servant in Edinburgh at the time, he narrates that the pipes were screaming out a stormy pibroch to the tune of "We'll awa to Sherramuir to haud the Whigs in order." He, however, tries human credulity too far in asserting that — notwithstanding the yells from a

---

[1] Culloden Papers, p. 224.
[2] Tales of a Grandfather, vol. ii. pp. 316, 318 *et seq.*
[3] Mahon's The '45, p. 45.
[4] Chambers's Hist., p. 96; Lockhart Papers, p. 488.

thousand Highland throats and the skirling of many bagpipes—the citizens slept till their usual hour of rising, and woke to find with surprise the transference of the government of the town. The official Jacobite account, published in their organ, the 'Caledonian Mercury' of the day, epitomised the subject by saying that after Charles had informed the magistrates that "he was come to enter his beloved metropolis, a deputation was sent out; the agreement made was not known, but early in the morning about 100 Highlanders peaceably entered the city." The use of the word "agreement" in this publication proves that loyal old Professor Maclaurin was justified in using the term "a plain collusion" when he described the transaction to Lord President Forbes, at Culloden.[1] The wish expressed by Sir Andrew Mitchell, Lord Tweeddale's secretary, that Cope would arrive in time to save the capital and hang the Lord Provost, was not fulfilled.

In the forenoon the Prince, having heard that all was safe in the city, marched with the main body of his troops round its southern side beyond the range of the castle guns to the valley between the hill called Arthur's Seat and Salisbury Crags. Leaving his men to encamp there, and accompanied

[1] Culloden Papers, p. 262.

by his chiefs and other men of rank, he proceeded to the royal Palace of Holyrood through the Park, which was filled with "vast numbers of people of all persuasions, who crowded to see the Chevalier."[1] Among these was John Home, the historian, who writes thus: "The figure and presence of Charles Stewart were not ill suited to his lofty pretensions. He was in the prime of youth, tall and handsome, and of a fair complexion. . . . He stood some time in the Park to show himself to the people, and then, though he was very near the palace, mounted his horse, either to render himself more conspicuous, or because he rode well, and looked graceful on horseback. The Jacobites were charmed with his appearance. They compared him to Robert Bruce, whom he resembled, they said, in his figure as in his fortune. The Whigs looked upon him with other eyes. They acknowledged that he was a goodly person; but they observed that even in that triumphant hour, when he was about to enter the palace of his fathers, the air of his countenance was languid and melancholy, and that he looked like a gentleman and man of fashion, but not like a hero or a conqueror. Hence they formed their conclusions that the enterprise was above the pitch

[1] Scots Magazine, 1745, p. 437.

of his mind, and that his heart was not great enough for the sphere in which he moved." A large body of armed men and an immense multitude of spectators surrounded the cross of Edinburgh when at midday the official heralds and pursuivants with all due pomp proclaimed James VIII. King of Scotland, and the Prince as Regent. The documents were dated at Rome, two years before, and had been prepared for the use of a previously intended enterprise. A manifesto of more recent date from Charles himself was also read. Upon this Home writes: "The populace of a great city, who huzza for anything that brings them together, huzzaed; and a number of ladies in the windows strained their voices with acclamation, and their arms with waving white handkerchiefs in honour of the day. These demonstrations of joy, among people of condition, were chiefly confined to one sex; few gentlemen were to be seen on the streets or in the windows; and even among the inferior people, many showed their dislike by a stubborn silence."[1] Carlyle also remarks that two-thirds of the men were friends, and two-thirds of the ladies were enemies, to Government.[2] In the manifesto ample promises were made for the free exercise of the Protestant religion; and, as remarked

---

[1] Home's Hist., vol. iii. p. 71. [2] Carlyle's Autobiography, p. 112.

by the Earl of Rosebery, "had Charles then been able to renounce Roman Catholicism, and anticipated by five years the abjuration of 1750, he might have swept Scotland. A name like that of Stuart, borne by a Protestant Prince, would have raised the nation in its cause; but religion outweighed all else." Lord Rosebery, however, seems to have attributed too lofty motives to the conduct of the Prince, who while within the British dominions appears to have paid little, if any, attention to the rites of the Church to which he nominally belonged.[1] He foiled the inquiries of his Highland friends as to what his real religion was, by telling them that some of the princes in Europe had good and some bad consciences, but that in reality they had little or no religion at all; and when seriously pressed by Keppoch and others, for the sake of his own interests in England, to join in divine worship with a Protestant clergyman, all the answer they could get was, "Pray, gentlemen, can you assure me that I will not be obliged to return to foreign parts? Satisfy me as to this point, and I will know what to do." This reply, too, was in marked contrast to his repeated and public boasts of being determined to conquer or die in his present

[1] Lyon in Mourning, vol. ii. p. 96; Ewald's Life of Prince Charles, p. 347.

enterprise. Lord Rosebery also remarks, that "it was not seventy years since the Young Chevalier's grandfather sat and gloated over the sufferings of the saints in the council chamber at Holyrood." But the Prince, in order to influence the Scottish people, would have had to attend service in the Presbyterian High Church of Edinburgh, while it was to make converts to Episcopalianism, not to Roman Catholicism, that James II., when Duke of York, had persecuted "the saints."

The two days following the capture of the capital were usefully occupied in refreshing with ample and wholesome food, "and cordials also," the Highlanders, who were now in high spirits, in improving their clothing and appointments, and in distributing the arms which had been surrendered. Even this supply, in addition to the weapons brought in the Doutelle, and those already in the possession of the clans, were not found sufficient to fully equip all the men now with the Prince. A party of Macgregors in particular, commanded by the double spy James Macgregor, eldest son of Rob Roy, are stated to have remained armed only with scythes tied on to stout staves. On the 18th Lord Nairne, another of the Murray clan, had arrived with 500 (some authorities say 1000) men, including the Maclauchlans with their chief.[1] It is difficult to ascertain the exact strength of the insurgents, as their numbers were systematically disguised and minimised by their leaders, with the object of causing little alarm to the existing Government. Some fifty gentlemen with their servants were formed into a small troop of horse, who, being well mounted, soon became very useful in scouting and other light cavalry duties. But few others joined the ranks; and even the Stuart partisans in the magistracy "ceased to appear in their proper habits."[2]

[1] Tales of a Grandfather, vol. iii. p. 6; Mahon's The '45, p. 48.
[2] Scots Magazine, 1745, p. 437.

CHAPTER VII.

SIR JOHN COPE landed at Dunbar on the 17th September, but the disembarkation of his troops was not completed till the 18th. He heard with surprise and concern of the capitulation of Edinburgh, and was disappointed that the promised Dutch regiments had not arrived. A council of war was held, at which Colonel Gardiner and others were in favour of delaying till their arrival. But these were not Cope's views, and on the 18th he wrote to Lord Tweeddale, " I march to-morrow morning, and will do the best I can for his Majesty's service." His resolution was formally approved of by the king. In the same letter the General reported having found at Dunbar Gardiner's and Hamilton's regiments, "extremely fatigued with the forced marches they had made." It may be doubted if he knew how very badly these dragoons had behaved; but Gardiner himself was not reticent on the subject. He was staying with the minister of the town, and on Wednesday was visited by his young friend Alexander Carlyle, who with John Home and others had made their way to Dunbar for the purpose of again tendering their services as volunteers. Although the Colonel was looking "pale and dejected," he received the lad with all his old kindness. On a hope being expressed that a good account might be given of the rebels, now that a junction of the foot with the dragoons had been effected, Gardiner remarked "that he hoped it might be so, but — and then he made a long pause." Again, when young Carlyle ventured to allude to what he called "the hasty retreat" from Prestonpans, which he had witnessed on the Monday night, the old soldier exclaimed: "A foul flight, Sandie, and they have not recovered from their panic; and I'll tell you in confidence that I have not above ten men in my regiment whom I am certain will follow me. But we must give them battle now, and God's will be done." He was quite unconscious that his own teaching and tactics had destroyed their natural courage. At dinner, however, at which the minister's family and Cornet Ker were present, he assumed an air of gaiety, and rallied Carlyle as a raw soldier on his little adventures of the previous night, "and spoke of victory as a thing certain, if God were on our side."[1] The other volunteer, whose name has been mentioned, John Home, had an interview with the General, and informed him that he had stayed in Edinburgh to count the rebels, whose numbers he was certain were not above 2000. The self-confident young man, unaccustomed to such calculations, must have been deceived; but his computation, tallying as it did with their own official account, and repeated in his History, written half a century afterwards, has been too often received as authoritative. But Cope had truer information. Before leaving Aberdeen he wrote to the Lord President that "the Young Chevalier had at most not above 4000 men at Perth"; and before he left Dunbar intelligence from Edinburgh reached him through Gardiner "that the enemy were 4000 strong, and if not fallen upon next day, they would be joined by more from the North."[2]

There can be no doubt as to the numbers of Cope's force. Exclusive of a small band of Highlanders of somewhat doubtful loyalty, he had about 600 horse and 1400 foot. The artillery consisted of six 1½-pounder galloper guns and six small mortars;

[1] Carlyle's Autobiography, p. 131; Cope's Trial, p. 191; Home's Hist., vol. iii. p. 76.
[2] Culloden Papers, p. 220; Henderson's Hist., p. 76; Cope's Trial, pp. 43, 59, 40, 157, 47.

but there were still no trained gunners. Cope's attention to details is shown by his unceasing but futile efforts to procure these men. In July he had pointed out their absolute necessity to Lord Tweeddale, and when he heard at Aberdeen of their having reached Edinburgh, he wrote ordering them to be held in readiness to meet him at his landing. From Dunbar he again wrote for them, and none coming, Lieutenant Craig volunteered to "risk himself" by carrying a message to General Guest, requesting that they might be sent at once along with the chief engineer. Craig, however, did not get within the gates of the castle till eleven o'clock on the night of Friday the 20th, and then Guest declined to spare the engineer; but, after making some difficulties, he handed over one bombardier and four gunners to the lieutenant. They were disguised as tradesmen, and at two o'clock on the Saturday morning were despatched with a guide to lead them to Sir John's camp, about ten miles distant, which they failed in reaching. Meanwhile Cope had borrowed from the men-of-war in Dunbar roads six sailor gunners, "who were generally drunk on the march, and ran away before the coming action began."

During the forenoon of Thursday the royal troops advanced about ten miles, and encamped on the rising ground to the west of Haddington. Cope had throughout the march ridden among the ranks, speaking so cheeringly to the men "that even the dragoons breathed nothing but revenge, and threatened the rebels with nothing but destruction."[1] The people of the country, however, flocked from all quarters to see the unwonted military display, and Carlyle, who rode along with Hamilton's regiment, remarks: "I was not acquainted with the discipline of armies; but it appeared to me to be very imprudent to allow all the common people to converse with the soldiers as they pleased, by which means the panic was kept up and perhaps their principles corrupted. Many people in East Lothian were Jacobites, and they were most forward to mix with the soldiers." An incident occurred during the afternoon which prevented the panic spirit from dying out, and, it may be, tended to infect the infantry with its malign influence. Carlyle's narrative describes its cause and effects. He "with the volunteers, twenty-five in number, assembled at the principal inn of Haddington, where also sundry officers of dragoons and staff came for their dinner. While our dinner was preparing an alarm was beat in the camp, which occasioned a great hurry-scurry in the

[1] Cope's Trial, pp. 51, 48; Home's Hist., vol. iii. p. 77; Carlyle's Autobiography, p. 133.

courtyard with the officers taking their horses, which some of them did with no small reluctance, either through love of their dinner or aversion to the enemy. I saw Colonel Gardiner passing very slowly, and ran to ask him what was the matter. He said it could be nothing but a false alarm." It had happened that the Hon. Francis Charteris, the rich younger brother of Lord Elcho and the supplier of the welcome, but never repaid, loan made by the latter to Prince Charles, had been married the day before at Prestonhall, a mansion about eight miles distant, to a daughter of the Duchess of Gordon. The bridal party, escorted by the usual little cavalcade, was proceeding to their house, which had recently been called New Amisfield, near Haddington. Alarming news of an approaching foe somehow accompanied their coach, and as their Jacobite sympathies were well known, the apprehension caused was believed to have been not altogether unintentional. Cope made the best of the awkward occurrence by thanking his troops for their alertness, and they, Colonel Whiteford mentions, "returned him a huzza." Everything the General did or did not do has been the object of the reckless criticism of both Jacobite and Hanoverian writers. For example, Sir Walter Scott bitterly ridicules him for not having on this day marched three miles farther west to Gladsmuir, and, encamping there, awaited an onslaught from the Prince. He affirms that the old soothsayer, who prophesied that

"On Gladsmuir shall the battle be,"

"had a better judgment for selecting a field of battle than Sir John Cope," and adds, "It must always be a subject of wonder that he did not halt to receive the Highlanders there, instead of cooping himself up in a pinfold at Preston and waiting for their attack."[1] But Sir John had no certainty that Charles would advance to meet him. The resolution to do so was not, in fact, formed till that evening; and Cope's instructions admitted of no delay. The evidence on the General's trial shows that he intended to have made his day's halt at Gladsmuir, and that he did not do so because he was truly informed that there was a scarcity of water there for men and animals. Moreover, the "muir" or moor was broken up by clumps of strong furze, which would have impeded the movements of his cavalry, and was so extensive that he would have been certainly outflanked by an enemy whom he knew to be of more than double his own numbers. The source of Sir Walter's remarks is shown by their being identical in statement, and occasionally in words, with those

---

[1] Tales of a Grandfather, vol. iii. p. 40; Murray of Broughton's Narrative, p. 21; Cope's Trial, p. 143.

of the traitor Murray. Mr Drummond, the zealous captain of the first company of late Edinburgh volunteers, came to Haddington in the afternoon, and proposed to Cope that those of his men who had joined should be formed into a company and given a station in the infantry line; but the General thought that for that evening at least those of them who were intimately acquainted with the county would be more usefully employed in reconnoitring on horseback the roads leading from the enemy to his camp. Two of these scouts, who afterwards became Lord Gardenstone and General Cunningham, leaving the camp at midnight, ventured to cross the Esk at Musselburgh, and shortly after daylight, when within four miles of the rebel camp, to enter Christal's hostelry. While regaling themselves with "white wine and oysters" they were captured by a Highland picket and conducted to the Chevalier's headquarters. There they fortunately met with personal friends. A threat of hanging them as spies was commuted into one of exposure in the forefront of battle to the fire of their friends; but finally they were allowed to slip away, and they rejoined the royal army in the afternoon. Scott attributes undue importance to this incident, by erroneously stating that Cope, from being deprived of the information expected from these scouts, was suddenly surprised by seeing his enemy occupying the ridge of an acclivity on his left near Preston.[1]

After breakfasting on the morning of Friday the 20th, Sir John resumed his march towards Edinburgh, having resolved, should the Prince not meet him on the road, "to form a strong camp" near Musselburgh, "in order to have but a little way" (five miles) "to march the next day before he attacked the rebels."[2] He had arranged with General Guest to breach the town walls with the castle guns, so as to admit, if deemed desirable, the entrance of the royal troops. The ground round the intended camp was well suited to the regular movements of both horse and foot, and covered in part the position occupied by the English two hundred years before at the battle of Pinkie, disastrous to the Scots. Lord Loudon, the adjutant-general, and Major Caulfield, the quartermaster-general, with Lord Drummore, whose estate marched with that of Pinkie, and other gentlemen rode on in advance to reconnoitre and mark off the proposed encampment. About three miles west of Haddington, which is seventeen miles from Edinburgh, the road to the capital divided and again united near Preston, about four miles short of the intended halting-ground. The southern and higher

[1] Tales of a Grandfather, vol. iii. p. 13; Home's Hist., vol. iii. p. 84; Quarterly Review. [2] Cope's Trial, pp. 36, 48, 137, 144.

branch runs along an almost level plateau from 300 to 400 feet above the sea as far as Tranent. The ground beyond that village towards Fawside Castle, till the road struck down to Preston at Birslie Brae, was at that time unfit for the movements of cavalry or infantry on account of its being broken up by hollow roads, coal-pits, and walls. The northern and lower road had none of these drawbacks, and yet historians treat with scorn Cope's military capacity because he wisely gave it the preference.[1] The greater portion of this day's march traversed the confiscated domains of the Setons, who from the days of Bruce had stood high among the leading families in Scotland, and whose last representative was now an impoverished exile. With hereditary loyalty to the Stuarts he had joined in the Rebellion of 1715, and after being captured and condemned to be beheaded, had saved himself from execution by effecting a daring escape from the Tower of London. The road passed on its right the steading of Garlton, the farm of Skirving, who was subsequently the witty author of "Hey! Johnnie Cope," and also the pleasant half ancient keep and half modern mansion of George Hamilton of Redhouse, who had just joined the Prince, and who paid the penalty of making a wrong choice by hanging at York in the

[1] Cope's Trial, pp. 144, 146.

following year. After marching about seven miles a short halt was ordered near the partly ruined " Palace of Seton," which had been successfully held by Brigadier Mackintosh against the force of the Duke of Argyll in the previous rising. It may be well to note that during this easy forenoon's march Colonel Gardiner was—to use the words of his biographer, Dr Doddridge—" in so weak a state that he could not well endure the fatigue of riding on horseback," which necessitated his being conveyed in a coach from Haddington. This sight must have damped what confidence his dragoons still retained regarding their commander's physical efficiency as a cavalry leader.

After a short halt at Seton the troops were about to resume their march to the proposed camp, five miles farther to the west, when Lord Loudon galloped back from the reconnoitring party with tidings that the Highlanders had already crossed the Esk at Musselburgh, and were in full march towards Preston, which would be reached by them before the royal forces could form on the open ground beyond the walled enclosures of the village. Cope has been severely blamed for not having now—while there was yet time—ascended from the lower plateau, on which Seton and Preston stand, to the higher but unsuitable locality of Tranent. This censure is misplaced. The

General had simply to clear himself from the small Seton village, when he found himself on a field "proper for his purpose"; and as described by himself, "there is not in the whole ground between Edinburgh and Dunbar a better spot for both horse and foot to act upon,"[1] or one, he might have added, more adapted by nature to the numbers and character of his troops. It extended somewhat over a mile and a quarter from east to west, where it was bounded on the outskirts of Preston by the thin but high park wall of Grange House, the home of George Erskine, commonly known as Lord Grange, the eccentric brother of the Earl of Marr, who commanded the Jacobite army in the last Rebellion. The breadth of the ground north and south was about a mile. Its southern half, on which the action next day took place, was nearly flat, while on the northern half a gentle fall of about 100 feet brought the surface down to the level of the link-covered shore, upon which stood the village of Cockenzie. A crop of wheat had just been gathered from the field, which was unbroken by ditch, wall, or hedge, and upon which one tree alone stood, and still stands, celebrated in the ballad as

> "The thorn-tree, which you may see,
> Bewest the Meadowmill, man."

---

[1] Cope's Trial, pp. 37, 53.

The road to Edinburgh ran along the south margin of the ground. Between it and the foot of the slope up to the higher plateau, on which Tranent stands, there lay a strip of partially reclaimed morass, the surplus waters of which, at its eastern extremity, flowed in a small stream through Seton to the sea. This "uncouth piece of ground," as Home calls it, was passable in three places. Near its east end there was a winding, unseen, and little-known footpath from a small valley near the farm of Rigganhead."[1] About the centre of its length it was crossed by the ordinary "very narrow" cart-road between Cockenzie and Tranent. A little farther west — a meadow with a mill intervening — an embankment, also "very narrow," traversed the flat for about 450 yards at its broadest part, and on it were a bridle-path and a tramway. These latter ran through the Heugh, then a wooded ravine, on the east bank of which stood the church and village of Tranent. The tramway was the oldest in Scotland, and had been made to carry coal from the ancient collieries on the higher lands to the salt-works and harbour at Cockenzie. The west portion of the old marsh had been for the most part reclaimed, but was cut up with ditches and covered with small enclosures, surrounded by dry-stone dykes, hedges,

[1] Cope's Trial, p. 137.

and low willow-trees. It was terminated on the west by the fields and park of Bankton, the house of Colonel Gardiner. The road to Edinburgh here narrowed to what was called a "defile," having a breadth of not more than some 20 feet, and winding for several hundred yards between the park walls of the Colonel and those of Lord Grange, till it reached the village of Preston.

Near the tramway, on the field thus described, Sir John Cope formed his little army, facing west, with the left flank resting on the broad ditch edging the morass, and the right extending northwards to the sea. The infantry had two guns in their centre and two on each extremity, and on each of the flanks were placed two squadrons of cavalry. His five Highland companies—"most of them very weak"—80 or 90 volunteers, still unarmed, and the remaining two squadrons of dragoons, constituted the reserve.[1] The line stood somewhat less than half a mile from the wall of Grange park, which stretched for about the same distance along its front; but Cope ordered a large part of this wall to be thrown down, in order that the enemy might be dislodged should they try to occupy the enclosures. Such an attempt could not be made without some loss of time, as the eccentric

[1] Cope's Trial, pp. 144, 172.

proprietor had, according to Carlyle, whose father's manse was close by, laid out "his fine gardens with close walks, labyrinths, and wildernesses, which, though it did not occupy above four or five acres, cost one at least two hours to perambulate."[1] The position taken up could be attacked in front through two "defiles," one passing, as has been mentioned, between the enclosures of Bankton and Grange House, and the other separating the latter from the orchards of the houses at the east end of Prestonpans. It was also feasible for the enemy to pass through the village nearer the shore, and to form for attack upon the then open links between Prestonpans and Cockenzie. But the first mode of onslaught was hazardous, and the last involved an advance up a slope, which the Highlanders did not like.

The reception accorded to the royal troops in East Lothian was very different from that experienced in Perthshire. Henderson records that "nothing was wanting for the conveniency of men or horses. The gentlemen supplied the officers with delicacies, and the private men with every proper refreshment, while the people joined to send them tuns of Scots beer and spirits, while workmen flocked in to enter upon the most difficult tasks upon the first orders."[2]

[1] Cope's Trial, pp. 38, 146, 138; Carlyle, p. 7.   [2] Henderson's Hist.

The Prince had given a splendid ball at Holyrood on the 17th, and on the next day had reviewed all his forces. He was fully acquainted with every detail of Cope's numbers and movements. On the 19th he learnt of his march to Haddington, and in the evening a council of war was held in the camp at Duddingston, which came to the unanimous conclusion that they had no choice as to marching forward next day and giving battle to the royal general. After this was settled Charles appears to have bluntly asked the chiefs how they expected their men to behave in action. This untoward question, put on such an occasion, displayed a want of confidence in the courage of his followers which must have given pain and displeasure to men whose lives and fortunes could only be saved by the success of the enterprise. Macdonald of Keppoch, being not only of high standing among them, but having also been trained in the French army, answered in their behalf that the gentlemen of every clan would lead the attack with gallantry into the midst of the enemy, and that the clansmen would certainly follow them with fidelity. Little did the chivalrous chieftain anticipate that before seven months were over the men in whom he so fully trusted would stubbornly refuse to follow him in the charge, and would coolly allow him to be shot to death with the exclamation on his lips, "My God! have the children of my tribe forsaken me"?[1] Nor does another incident, which occurred shortly before the troops marched on the 20th, indicate either heart or tact on the Prince's part. Grant of Glenmorriston, by making a night march, had joined the force with his men. Travel-soiled and unshaven, he hurried into the Chevalier's presence. He was welcomed with no thanks for his zeal, but with a sarcastic remark on the rugged condition of his chin. Glenmorriston turned away with kindling wrath, saying, "Sir, it is not beardless boys who are to do your business."

The Prince and his chiefs slept on the night of the 19th in houses near Duddingston, where his hardy mountaineers were bivouacking. Early in the morning the Highland guards, about 1000 strong, were withdrawn from Edinburgh; and it may be here remarked that General Guest did not consider it to be his duty to reoccupy the city, spike the cannon on the walls, or do any other action to render difficult or unpleasant the Prince's return to Holyrood and the capital. After breakfasting, the army marched in its usual column of threes for nearly four miles,

---

[1] Tales of a Grandfather, vol. iii. p. 8 *et seq.;* Chambers's Hist., pp. 298, 113; Mahon, The '45, p. 49; Ewald's Life of Prince Charles, p. 120.

when it crossed the Esk at Musselburgh bridge. The rivalry of the clans for the foremost place had been decided by lot in favour of the Camerons. This deeply offended the Macdonalds, who ever since the days of Bannockburn had asserted a claim to be on the right of a Scottish host on the day of battle. Lord Mahon states that the march was interrupted by straggling shots from the castle, which was two miles away, with a hill intervening; and Ewald with equally romantic fancy eulogises "the prudent generalship" of the Prince in keeping the high ground towards Musselburgh. The fact was that no precautions were either needed or taken, as the distance of the royal troops was perfectly known, and as the Esk, bridgeless from Dalkeith to Musselburgh, covered the right flank. Sir Walter Scott, following the erroneous topographical nomenclature of Murray of Broughton and other Jacobite writers, and copied by most succeeding historians, states that after crossing the Esk the Highlanders ascended Carberry Hill.[1] In reality they left that historical eminence above two miles on their right, and marched by the south of Pinkie gardens along the ordinary road towards Preston, till they came,

[1] Scott's Tales, &c., vol. iii. p. 11; Murray of Broughton's Narrative p. 19; Lord George Murray in Chambers's Jacobite Memoirs, p. 36.

about a mile west of that village, near to Wallyford. Lord George Murray led the van, and states that he there received "certain information that Sir John Cope was at or near Preston, and that in all appearance he would endeavour to gain the high ground of Fawside. There was no time to deliberate or wait for orders. I was very well acquainted with the grounds, and as I was confident that nothing could be done to purpose except the Highlanders got above the enemy, I struck off to the right through the fields, without holding any road. In less than half an hour, by marching quick, I got to the eminence. I went very slow, after I got possession of the ground, till the rear was fully joined. We then marched in order towards Tranent, and all the way in sight of the enemy." Cope had, however, as has been mentioned, determined not to occupy this high ground, and Lord George's erroneous surmise that he would do so resulted in the ensuing events having the character of a chapter of accidents rather than that of thought-out plans. As the Highlanders marched up the ascent to Fawside they had been carefully counted by Lieutenant Craig of Wynyard's, the 17th, Regiment, who estimated them at upwards of 5000 men. These numbers correspond with those derived from other sources. Cope, on his part, came to the conclusion that the rebels had chosen their present ground on account of its being so broken up that his cavalry could not act upon it; but on observing their movements he formed his line of battle so as to face the enemy, with his left resting on the tram or waggon way and his right extending westward towards Lord Grange's park wall. The wide ditch of the morass covered the whole of his front.[1]

It was now past two o'clock. The weather was fine and the sun shone bright. Only half a mile separated the two armies, on the defeat of one or other of which the possession of Scotland, for a time at least, was staked. The Highlanders, arrayed along the edge of the eminence about 150 feet above the plain, could count their antagonists, and though impressed by the brilliant show below them, and by the regular movements of the king's troops, they could confide in their own superior numbers and in the apparent advantage, which at first sight their position gave them, of being able to charge down-hill upon their foe. Every historian dwells on the huzzas, by some called "shouts and yells of defiance," which were

---

[1] Cope's Trial (evidences of Lieutenant Craig, Mr" Baillie, Colonel Whiteford, Majors Talbot and Severn, and Captain Leslie), p. 59; Duke of Perth's statements.

exchanged between the adversaries. Much importance was still attached to the energy of these challenges. At Killiecrankie, when in 1689 similar forces opposed one another, the military shout of the soldiers was marked as being dull and sullen compared to the yell of the Highlanders; and Sir Evan Cameron of Lochiel called attention to the fact, saying that "in all his battles he observed victory had ever been on the side of those whose shout before joining seemed most sprightly and confident."[1] On the present occasion, it is asserted, "the huzza of the Royalists, particularly that of the dragoons, was much louder than that of the enemy," which Henderson attributes to there being a sort of panic visible among the private men of the rebels," caused from "their observation of the coldness of the country people toward them, and from a consciousness of the doubtful fortune of war." There was, however, a more potent reason for their conduct and for the pause in the action of the forces. The partial local knowledge of Lord George Murray, who virtually directed most of the military operations of the rebels, had enabled him to gain a position above the king's troops; but until he scanned from a short distance the intervening piece of ground lying at the foot of the slope, he

[1] Henderson's Hist., p. 78; Green's Reading, p. 40.

was unaware of its real character.[1] It had nothing formidable in its look to catch the eye of a casual passer-by. He and the other leaders now saw that it was cut up, as has been described, by hedges, dry-stone walls, and ditches, which would break the impetus given by the descent to any column attempting to charge through it, and destroy all military formation, while the men would be exposed to unanswered volleys of musketry from the farther bank. Chevalier de Johnstone, Lord George's aide-de-camp, whose narrative, though in some parts obviously inaccurate, may on this matter be deemed reliable, describes the effect produced on the Highlanders by "a full view of the position of Sir John Cope, which was chosen with a good deal of skill. The more we examined it, the more we were convinced of the impossibility of attacking it, and we were all thrown into consternation, and quite at a loss what course to take. The camp of the enemy was fortified by nature, and in the happiest position for so small an army. . . . We spent the afternoon in reconnoitring his position, and our uneasiness and chagrin increased as we saw no possibility of attacking it without exposing ourselves to be cut to pieces

[1] Letter from Lord George Murray to Hamilton of Bangour, 'Home's Hist.,' vol. iii. p. 365.

in a disgraceful manner." The Jacobite official account of the battle, and the narratives of the two Highland officers in the 'Lockhart Papers,' admit that the generalship of their commander was foiled, and that "nothing less than authority restrained the clansmen from running down upon the enemy and coming to action directly."[1] Serious dissension and controversy arose as to what was to be done, to end which Lord George Murray despatched Colonel Ker of Graden, who had field experiences in the Spanish army, to descend and observe well the "uncouth" ground. Mounted on a little white pony, he performed this duty with perfect coolness under a scattered fire of muskets from Cope's skirmishers, and reported that a direct attack was impracticable. His decided opinion coinciding with that of Mr Robert Anderson, younger of Whitburgh, and of other local people, the idea of a direct attack was abandoned. Some confusion in the personal direction of operations seems also to have arisen. Murray of Broughton, in his garbled narrative, complains of the Prince not having been made acquainted with orders afterwards given by Lord George, in which he was

[1] Memoirs of the Rebellion by Chevalier de Johnstone, p. 23; Lockhart Papers, pp. 448, 489; Gentleman's Magazine, p. 517; Lord George Murray in Jacobite Papers, p. 37.

obliged unwillingly to acquiesce; and Lord George himself strongly resents the interference of Colonel O'Sullivan, the Irish quartermaster-general, in having without his knowledge, but doubtless with the sanction of the Prince, sent a detachment of Camerons to occupy the churchyard at the foot of the then wooded heugh or ravine before mentioned, which was, he thought, in too close proximity to the king's troops.[1] This movement was not, however, perceived until Mr Grosset, the active Government official who was now scouting for Cope, ventured to penetrate the ravine, and received a fire from the churchyard on the one side and from the brushwood on the other. The muskets then in use were not arms of precision, and the shooting was as ineffective as that which had been directed against Colonel Ker. On Mr Grosset's return about four in the afternoon, Sir John Cope directed Colonel Whiteford to advance two of the galloper guns and to open fire upon the churchyard, which was only 830 yards distant. The effect was good, and some of the Camerons were soon disabled. Lord George records that the king's troops huzzaed at every discharge; and Lochiel himself, being summoned to the spot, returned with the report "that

---

[1] Murray of Broughton's Narrative, p. 20; Home's Hist., vol. iii. p. 87; Jacobite Memoirs, p. 37; Cope's Trial, p. 88.

nothing could dishearten men more than to be placed in an open exposed part where they could not advance." Murray authorised their withdrawal, and meeting Colonel O'Sullivan shortly after in the middle of the village of Tranent, an animated altercation on the subject took place, in which, needless to say, his lordship had the mastery.

Meanwhile a party of Highlanders was detached to descend by a hollow road and quarry to the ground south of Gardiner's house, which was then taken possession of by Cope's troops, and occasional brisk firing took place in its neighbourhood till nightfall.[1] A little incident occurred during the afternoon, which, though somewhat of a domestic nature, may perhaps be worth narrating. Charles, when moving about with his personal staff, happened to pause near the house of Mr Anderson of Windygoul, the aged uncle of the Robert Anderson already mentioned, and who was destined to play an important part in future operations. Members of the family had been "out in the '15," and they were still loyal Jacobites. Knowing of whom the group must be composed, the old gentleman desired his eldest daughter to take refreshments on a salver to the Prince. But the damsel was "blate," and a younger sister volunteered to do

[1] Cope's Trial, pp. 138, 39.

the duty. Charles drank a glass of wine, and acknowledged the hospitality not only with thanks but also by giving a hearty kiss to the comely lass. The family tradition runs, that on seeing and hearing this, the elder sister remarked, "Eh, but I had kent!"[1]

About five o'clock the rebels, taking advantage of their position and superior numbers, divided their army into two bodies, sending one along the brow of the plateau a short distance to the east, and the other, including the Atholl brigade, to the west and north, by which they seemed to intend taking possession of Prestonpans and utilising the north-west entrances to the field occupied by the royal army. To meet this threatened attack Cope, sending his baggage to the precincts of Cockenzie House, formed line obliquely across the plain. The enemy's movements being concealed by interjacent trees and gardens, he used some of his volunteers as scouts, young Carlyle among them being stationed as a look-out on the little steeple of his father's church. This portion of the Highland army was then withdrawn, and fell back to its original position on the brow of the plateau to the west of Tranent. As they had never gone far from the base of the slope, it may be gathered that the objects of the movement were to

---

[1] *Anglicè*, "Oh, if I had but known!"

occupy the impatient men, and to puzzle Cope with regard to the rebel plans, while probably a hope was entertained that the royal general might be tempted into leaving his favourable position to fall upon an apparently detached portion of the Prince's army. On the retirement of the enemy from his right flank, Cope resumed his second line of battle facing the south, a short distance in rear of the ditch extending east and west along the morass, with his left resting on the waggon-way, and his right stretching towards the park walls of Grange House.[1]

About this time Lord George Murray, having entered Tranent, sent to inform the Prince, who apparently had gone to the rear, that he was sure the only way to come at the enemy was from the east side of Tranent. Lord George states, "I desired Lochiel to march these men," who had been removed from the churchyard, "through the village" (eastwards), "and that I should march the line and join them." He adds: "I told Mr O'Sullivan," whom he had met in the village, "that it was not possible to attack the enemy from the west, that the men he had placed at the foot of the village were exposed to no purpose, and that as there were exceedingly good

---

[1] Carlyle's Autobiography, p. 139; Jacobite Memoirs, p. 38; Cope's Trial, p. 146.

fields on the east side for the men to lie well and safe all that night, I should satisfy his Royal Highness how easy it would be to attack the enemy by the east side. I took the ground I designed; and when all were past the village except the Atholl brigade, who were to continue on the west side above Colonel Gardiner's enclosures, his Royal Highness came to the front of the line. The men lay down in rank and file. The place was perfectly dry, with stubble. . . . It was now night, and when all the principal officers were called together, I proposed attacking the enemy at break of day. I assured them that it was not only practicable, but that it would in all probability be attended with success. I told them I knew the ground myself, and had a gentleman or two with me who knew every part thereabouts." He then at length explained his plan to them, and adds, "The Prince was highly pleased, as indeed the whole officers were; so, after placing a few pickets, everybody lay down at their posts, and supped upon what they had with them."[1] Murray's plan was doubtless to gain access to the plain before daylight by making a short circuit round the east end of the marsh. This could easily have been done, as within half a mile of his present right flank a good paved

[1] Home's Hist., vol. iii. p. 87.

road, called Winton Loan, ran from the south-west tower of the gardens of Seton Palace to Winton Castle, another mansion of the great Seton family, situated about four miles to the south. By following it northwards for less than half a mile the main road could be reached, and another movement of no longer distance through the afterwards erased village of Seton would have brought him on to the field on which Cope's troops stood. The route had one disadvantage, as close to Seton there was a "defile" or narrow road between two stone walls which might have been blocked at its exit.

Young Anderson of Whitburgh had been present at the council of chiefs. He was too modest to bring forward his own views, but before he lay down for the night he told his old friend Colonel Hepburn of Keith, a chivalrous East Lothian gentleman who had joined the Prince at Holyrood, that having shot snipe in the marsh from boyhood, he knew well a pathway, now dry, which led direct from their right flank across the east end of the morass to the plain below. The movement of troops upon it, he was sure, could not be observed; and by using it, not only would time and distance and the passage of the defile at Seton be saved, but the men could be formed without being exposed to fire. On Hepburn's approving of the idea, Anderson asked him to come with him to communicate the information to Lord George Murray; but the old soldier, knowing that Murray's imperious nature made him apt to resent advice tendered by those at all equal to himself in rank, urged the young man to go alone. He ventured to do so, and found the leader already asleep upon the ground among a group of chiefs. On being awakened Lord George at once grasped the importance of the proposal. No time was lost in reconnoitring the path, and on its being found to accord with Anderson's description, Murray, taking Anderson with him, awoke the Prince, who, much pleased with the plan, ordered Lochiel and the other chieftains to be called. They in turn gave their full assent to the scheme.

Cope's troops also "lay on their arms" for the night in their last formation — except the little corps of 80 or 90 volunteers, who were to have been armed next morning, and who, on account probably of many of them not having greatcoats or other coverings to protect them from the cold, were dismissed to find quarters in the neighbouring villages, with directions to be upon the ground at daybreak, when they were to be allotted a place in the line of battle.[1] But, as

[1] Cope's Trial, p. 102.

testified at Cope's trial by their commander, Mr Drummond, their keeping the rendezvous was rendered impossible, as the action next morning began before daylight. These facts, however, have not saved them from being held up to ridicule as cowards, on the charge of having abandoned the field without orders. The five companies of Highlanders, which had formed till evening a portion of the reserve line, were now ordered to relieve at Cockenzie House the soldiers of the regular regiments, who had hitherto guarded the military chest and baggage. Knowing that the sympathies of many of the clansmen were naturally on the enemy's side, Cope prudently thought that their absence might be more useful than their presence in action.[1]

[1] Cope's Trial, pp. 102, 40, 132, 172.

CHAPTER VIII.

ALTHOUGH Sir John's plans had not been fully carried out, and the fight which he desired on ground suited to his force had not as yet taken place, he and his men had no reason to be dissatisfied with the day's proceedings. The enemy had been foiled in their tactics, and portions of their army had retired after making threatening advances. Cope's troops, though composed, with the exception of the cavalry and a few of the infantry, of young soldiers, had manœuvred with a steadiness which impressed his adversaries, and had lain down to sleep in excellent spirits. Yet Dr Doddridge, in his Life of Colonel Gardiner, which has universally been treated as containing historical facts, founds upon the later occurrences of the day a serious charge against the capacity of the General, and throws upon him individually the whole blame of the coming catastrophe, because he did not assent to the alleged solicitations of the Colonel to advance through the defiles and enclosures of Preston, and to attack the wing of the rebels which shortly before sunset had threatened his right flank.[1] If Colonel Gardiner was really thus urgently forward with his advice, it was strange on the part of one who, according to the reverend biographer himself, had to others besides young Carlyle expressed his belief that his own men would desert him on the day of battle. Lord Drummore, who with the Lord Advocate and the Solicitor-General had been on the field till after darkness came on, alludes, in a letter written to Cope in the following month, to "the thing" (such an attack) "having been under deliberation," and, with full local knowledge, gives the strongest reasons against it. It would, indeed, have been suicidal for the royal general to have abandoned a field on which his tiny force had ample room to act with freedom and effect, for one chosen by his foe on account of its possessing none of these advantages. Had Cope been so weak as to follow the proposal, the Highlanders from their right would have poured on to the plain as soon as he was actively engaged, and the result must have been immediate disaster. Dr Doddridge further states that on

---

[1] Henderson's Hist., p. 80; Cope's Trial, pp. 144, 146, 148; Jacobite officers' account, in 'Caledonian Mercury' and 'Gentleman's Magazine' for 1745, p. 517; Doddridge's Life, p. 142.

Gardiner's "unusually earnest insistance" on the foregoing suggestion "he dropped some earnest intimations" of the consequences which he apprehended, and which did "in fact follow." It is to be hoped that he was not guilty of the military crime of spreading despondency among his comrades. Carlyle gives no support to the credulous doctor's stories, but says that late in the evening "I visited Colonel Gardiner for the third time that day on his post, and found him grave, but serene and resigned; and he concluded by praying God to bless me, and added that he could not wish for a better night to lie on the field. He then called for his cloak and other conveniences for lying down, as he said that they would be awaked early enough in the morning."[1] Gardiner, Brigadier Fowke, Captain Singleton, Lord Home, and Lieutenant Wemyss, formed the group of officers who lay down together on the right of his own regiment.[2]

Another calumny must here be disposed of. Chambers, in his 'History of the Rebellion,' written eighty years after the events, was the first to publish the libel that Cope spent the night at Cockenzie, about a mile distant from his line of battle; and subsequent writers,

---

[1] Carlyle's Autobiography, p. 140.   [2] Cope's Trial, p. 79.

including Mahon, Ewald, and Veitch, eagerly dwell on the occurrence, which, if true, would constitute a shameful military offence. Ewald says: "Charles contented himself with the broad canopy of heaven, a shakedown of pease-straw, and the shoulder of a Highlander for a pillow; while the more luxurious Cope retired to comfortable quarters at Cockenzie."[1] During his month of campaigning, this was the first, or almost the first, occasion on which the Prince had not been able to secure for himself "comfortable quarters," while his men were for the most part bivouacking; and if any of these writers had taken the trouble to read either the Culloden Papers or the Proceedings of Cope's Trial, they would have found ample proof that Sir John slept that night with his soldiers on the field. General R. Wightman, writing to President Forbes five days afterwards, mentions that he himself, with Lord Drummore and Mr Drummond, the commander of the volunteers, was among those who found quarters at Cockenzie, and he makes no mention of Cope being there. Lord Drummore, in a letter to Cope written in the following month, alludes to having slept there, and to having "left you at eight o'clock

[1] Chambers's Hist., p. 125; Mahon's The '45, p. 52; Ewald's Life of Prince Charles, p. 122; Blackwood's Magazine, July 1894, p. 99.

at night lying upon your arms." Lord Stair mentions that Lord Loudon had written to him "immediately after the action, giving a full and circumstantial account of the affair," in which he spoke "very advantageously of Sir John Cope's personal behaviour, and particularly of his having been very alert all the night before the battle." Colonel Lascelles, who was acting as a brigadier, states: "About half-past two in the morning of the 21st, Lieutenant-Colonel Halket and I walked along the line, and by means of the large fire in front we saw the Earl of Loudon, and attended him to the General, acquainting him with what I had done," &c. Cope himself says: "To do the dragoons justice, they were very alert, and their patrols brought good intelligence the whole night of every motion the enemy made."[1] This statement he could not have ventured to make publicly in the presence of upwards of twenty officers who had been on the field, and who were called to point out any error in it, had he himself been sleeping in "comfortable quarters" at a mile's distance.

It was impossible for Sir John to station a fighting body of troops at every place where the enemy might attack; but he placed at sufficient distances all round his bivouac strong out-guards to prevent surprise, and

[1] Culloden Papers, p. 224; Cope's Trial, pp. 146, 52, 40, 66.

give time for his line to face the foe from whatever direction they chose to advance. He had large fires lit in front, which would have exposed to view any party attempting stealthily to make their way through the "uncouth ground" under cover of the darkness. Further to disturb those on the rising ground opposite, he directed shells to be thrown from the cohorn mortars.[1] This, however, he had to countermand, as, to use the expression of Mr Griffith, the old master gunner, "many of the fuzes had become damnified from long storage in Edinburgh Castle." The fall of such shells without bursting might have done away with the Highlanders' dread of their fatal effect. In addition to these precautions the General placed "a grand guard" of 100 dragoons on his left flank, whence the attack actually came. Of these the captain with 40 men watched the cart-road from Cockenzie to Tranent, 30 with the lieutenant were stationed along the morass eastwards, and the remaining 30 with the cornet were pushed forward to near Seton. These parties are stated to have sent patrols all night across the marsh close up to the enemy, who had, according to Lord George Murray, thrown out only a few pickets near their sleeping line. From dusk in the evening till eight o'clock, when darkness had come on, "a pretty brisk

[1] Cope's Trial, pp. 49, 91.

fire" was kept up by the rebels from the slope of the eminence on the south-east of Colonel Gardiner's house, and about nine o'clock "all the dogs in Tranent began to bark with the utmost fury, which continued till about half-past ten."[1] The royal officers correctly surmised that this clamour was occasioned by the bulk of the enemy passing through the village to the ground on the east. Cope states that "about three in the morning the patrols reported that the rebels were moving towards the east." This was the change (to be presently referred to) made in the formation of the Prince's army by the Macdonalds being brought from the left to the right of the column. It gave rise to the thought in the royal camp for a short time that the enemy were "going off" entirely from the ground. The whole line of foot were, however, at once ordered "to stand to their arms." Cope adds: "This report continued till about four. Then an account was brought us that they were moving northward, down towards Seton, to come by the east end of the plain, to attack us upon our left flank: upon which I immediately ordered the line to change its situation."[2]

In point of fact, his enemy was not moving to Seton, but to the end of the plain between that place and the

[1] Cope's Trial, pp. 65, 40.   [2] Ibid., pp. 139, 67.

royal line. From the wording of Cope's statement, from his having previously stated that the cavalry sent patrols across the morass, which was impracticable for mounted men except on the roads, and from the narrations of various officers, it seems probable that, though Cope had with him such local men as Gardiner and Lord Drummore, they were all unaware of the path made known by the sportsman Anderson to the rebel leaders. It appears to have been concluded that the Prince was marching round the farther end of the marsh instead of taking a short cut through. Had the existence of this path not been by a lucky chance divulged by one man to Prince Charles, Cope would have had at least three-quarters of an hour longer in which to shift the disposition of his troops and to familiarise them with their new ground. He would, moreover, have had the immense advantage of daylight. Sir John never admitted that he was taken by surprise, and in the strictly military sense of the term he was right. His men were completely formed in due battle array on good ground before his foe was upon him. But every one under him, and doubtless he himself, must have been puzzled and surprised by the sudden apparition, from the darkness and mist, of the enemy, who, they thought, could not attack them before daylight would show all their movements.

This unexpected scene, along with other unlooked-for circumstances, must have tended to unsettle the minds of his young infantry soldiers. The cavalry had already exhibited mental demoralisation.

Sir John Cope, as has been said, after hearing that the rebel column had headed northwards, lost none of the short time at his disposal. He at once shifted the frontage of his line. The men were in excellent spirits, and the necessary movements, which were executed by "the whole foot wheeling to the left by platoons," led by Major Talbot, were made without confusion. Lieutenant-Colonel (afterwards Sir Peter) Halkett of Lee's regiment mentions, however, in a marginal note on his copy of Cope's Trial: "It was so dark that I could not distinguish one of the pickets, who was marching within twenty-five paces, who they were." Meanwhile the staff officers were busy in calling in the out-guards. Among them was Major Caulfield, who in a letter to Cope states: "The last orders I received from you were to hasten in any of our parties that might still be out; and mistaking a body of Highlanders" (who had already crossed the marsh) "on their march in the dusk for a party of ours, I rid too near them, but returned and pointed them out to our artillery." In the new formation facing the east, Sir John's right rested on the cottages of the Meadowmill between the waggon-way and the cart-road leading from Cockenzie to Tranent.[1] On the extremity of this flank was posted the artillery guard, consisting of 100 men of Murray's regiment under Captain Cochran and Lieutenant Cranston. At an interval of ten yards on their left were aligned the six small mortars under the special charge of sturdy old Master Gunner Griffith, and the six little galloper guns.[2] Both mortars and guns were arranged at distances of only six feet apart, and all were commanded by Lieutenant-Colonel Whiteford.[3] A space was reserved between the cannon and the infantry for two squadrons of Gardiner's regiment, and then, stretching towards Cockenzie, there were in succession formed the five companies of Lee's, two companies of Guise's, the eight companies of Lascelles's, the remainder of Murray's regiment, and two squadrons of Hamilton's dragoons. The reserve, drawn up in a second line, consisted of a squadron from each of the cavalry regiments. Cope's object in making as extended a front as possible was apparently to prevent his being outflanked by his more numerous enemy. From the position of his extreme left the ground fell with a slightly more abrupt slope towards the sea. When the out-guards,

[1] Cope's Trial, p. 139.   [2] Ibid., pp. 91, 90.   [3] Ibid., p. 90.

consisting in all of 300 men, returned, there was not time to separate and send them to their respective corps. They were therefore formed to the right of Lee's regiment on a portion of the ground intended for the two squadrons of Gardiner's horsemen. Officers from every portion of the force testified at Cope's trial that the troops were fully formed before the attack began.[1]

Before daybreak the cavalry had been ordered to mount, and as soon as the formation of the infantry was complete, Cope sent directions to Brigadier Fowke to move up the dragoons. The brigadier accompanied the two squadrons of Gardiner's regiment to take up their allotted station on the right of the foot; but as the out-guards had been formed up on a part of the ground, there was not full space left for both squadrons, and therefore only that commanded by Lieutenant-Colonel Whitney was placed on the alignment, while that led by Colonel Gardiner himself was drawn up in rear with the guns in front of their right.[2] The brigadier states that "during the short time we had before joining the foot, I took an opportunity of assuring the squadrons that I had not the least doubt but that their behaviour that day would do us honour, and that our success

---

[1] Cope's Trial, p. 54.   [2] Ibid., p. 72.

would in a great measure be owing to their conduct." It may be mentioned that the Earl of Home stated at Cope's trial that, on the command to draw swords being given, Gardiner's horse became so troublesome that he advised the Colonel to take another horse, which from the rapid onset of the enemy must have been practically impossible.[1] The object in recording this detail in the Proceedings can only be surmised. Where possible, a marked reserve is maintained regarding this officer on the last two days of his life. He had on the 21st, as on the previous day, been appointed by Sir John to act as brigadier in command of the left wing of the force.[2] Colonel Lascelles was ordered to perform a similar office on the right, and was thus intrusted with new and more important duties on the morning of the action. Gardiner is recorded as remaining with only one squadron of his regiment on the right. Cope, without making any reflection on the missing officer, says that he himself posted Hamilton's dragoons on the left, a duty which would have been taken by a brigadier had he been present.[3] The rebels being then in sight and advancing, the General rode by the front of his line to the right, encouraging the men as he went along to do their duty, not to reserve their

---

[1] Cope's Trial, p. 81.   [2] Ibid., pp. 38, 44.   [3] Ibid., p. 41.

fire, and to be attentive to their officers.[1] In a cheap Jacobite contemporary account of the action, which doubtless had immense circulation, Cope, "the usurper's general," is falsely stated to have now promised his soldiers eight hours' plunder and pillage of Edinburgh after winning the expected victory.[2]

It has been mentioned that when, on the night of the 20th, the portion of the Highland army which was on the following morning to constitute their front line lay down to rest on the east side of Tranent, the Atholl brigade, destined to form their second line or *corps de reserve*, was left on the west side of that village, on the rising ground to the south of Colonel Gardiner's house. Murray of Broughton reduces the number of this strong brigade to 500 men, and states that the object of their being separated by the Prince was to intercept Cope should he attempt to move off to Edinburgh without fighting. Lord George Murray, however, specifically claims for himself the whole of the planning and carrying out of these operations; and he, apparently without even consulting Charles, ordered the Atholl brigade to come off its position at two o'clock, and "without the least noise" to join the rest of the force, which

[1] Cope's Trial, pp. 41, 61.   [2] Balmerino's Pamphlet, p. 2.

they did in good time, just before the northward march across the marsh began.[1] Broughton states that when the Prince discovered the recall of the Atholl brigade, he was so much displeased that "he at first seemed resolved to make them return," but that on reflection, in order to avoid occasioning "any confusion or distrust amongst his own people, he judged it safer and better to put up with the disappointment and continue the rest of his plan, though he could not help complaining that his orders had been neglected in so material a point." Before the advance on the 21st it had been necessary to make another alteration in the arrangement of the Highland army. The clan Cameron on the 20th obtained by lot the honour of leading the van and forming the right of the line—a distinction jealously claimed as their special right by the Macdonalds ever since the time of Bruce. Scott states that "the sagacity of Lochiel now induced the other chiefs to resign" to the claimants the coveted precedence, but Lord George Murray's simple statement is, that this change was made "according to what was agreed formerly upon."[2] Accordingly, at three in the morning, under the direction of Colonel

[1] Lord George Murray in Jacobite Memoirs, p. 38; and in letter to Hamilton of Bangour, Home's Hist., vol. iii. p. 353; Murray of Broughton's Narrative, p. 20.

[2] Tales of a Grandfather, vol. iii. p. 20; Jacobite Memoirs, p. 39.

Ker, the Macdonalds, headed by young Clanranald, filed from left to right along the front of the line, and thence were guided through the morass by Anderson, who was now attached to the staff of the Duke of Perth, the commander of the right wing of the Prince's front line. This nocturnal marching suited the genius and training of the Highlanders, and was effected in silence without confusion. As another precaution against noise, the horses of the mounted officers, from the Prince downwards, were left behind. It was thought that by this foresight and care the movements had been concealed from the enemy's observation, and doubtless this feeling inspired the rebel ranks with a certain amount of useful confidence; but, as has been mentioned, Cope's mounted patrols had watched and reported the various changes of position. The small body of insurgent cavalry under Lord Strathallan was left in the rear. Lord George Murray expressly states, "We brought no horse, to prevent being discovered by their noise." Murray of Broughton, however, anxious to have a hit at Lord George, apparently attributes their being left to his lordship's negligence; and Sir Walter Scott, disinclined to admit any fault in the rebel strategy, boldly affirms that they were duly "appointed to keep the height above the morass, that they might do what their numbers permitted to improve the victory," if the day was won.[1]

The passage through the marsh, which could not have been attempted in daylight, was safely accomplished, though not without some confusion and difficulty. The Prince himself fell in leaping the ditch. Scott censures Cope for not "having placed guns so as to enfilade this important pass, and for having no sentinel or patrol to observe the motions of the Highlanders in that direction." As to the latter charge, it has been shown that Sir John had, in fact, placed strong patrols along the edge of the morass; and as to the first, Sir Walter merely adopts Broughton's inimical narrative.[2] It would have been folly, indeed, on the royal general's part had he detached two or three from his six almost unmanned little cannon to the distance of about half a mile from his own line, even had he been aware of the existence of the path, of which he was, through no fault of his own, apparently ignorant.

On reaching firm ground the Duke of Perth, with the Macdonald regiments of Clanranald and Glengarry, and of Keppoch and Glencoe (united), continued to

[1] Jacobite Memoirs, p. 39; Murray of Broughton's Narrative, p. 202; Tales of a Grandfather, vol. iii. p. 21.

[2] Tales of a Grandfather, vol. iii. p. 21; Murray of Broughton's Narrative, p. 208.

march northwards, in order to give space for the remainder of the front line, the left wing of which, consisting of the Duke's own regiment and Macgregors, the Stewarts of Appin and the Camerons, was commanded by Lord George Murray. In this movement Perth, not being yet able in the half darkness and mist of the morning to see the formation of Cope's force, against which he did not wish to stumble, inclined somewhat eastwards to his right, a movement which caused the distance of the rebel right to be greater than that of their left from the royal army.[1] He marched also a little too far to the north before halting and facing his wing to the enemy, by which he unintentionally outflanked Cope's left. Lord George states: "After we had all passed the defile, I found (being in rear and to have command of the left) that the front had advanced too far. When we were passed about a hundred paces from the ditch, I immediately concluded, if we went further we should leave the enemy upon our left flank." A dangerous space would thus be left open in which the royal cavalry could act on his flank during the coming attack. He adds: "I therefore called to face the left, and the word was passed from the left to the right. We immediately marched on to the attack." Lord George also sent an

[1] Lockhart Papers, pp. 449, 490; Jacobite Memoirs, p. 39.

aide-de-camp to tell the Duke of Perth that it was time for the right to move, as the left was already advancing against the enemy. On his way to carry out the mission this officer met Anderson, who had been despatched by the Duke to say that his wing was ready to march. The left had thus the start of the right in what was intended to have been a simultaneous movement. Prince Charles did not attempt to exercise any general command. This is an example of the haphazard style in which the fighting in this Rebellion was conducted.[1]

At the same time the second line or reserve had likewise passed the marsh. It was composed principally of the Atholl brigade—*i.e.*, the regiments of Lord George Murray, Lord Nairn, and Menzies of Shian—and was, according to Broughton, "commanded by my L[ord] R[egent, Prince Charles]." The official, and almost all historical, accounts record that the Prince now addressed his troops in these words: "Follow me, gentlemen, and by the blessing of God I will make you a free and happy people!" But as the Prince did

---

[1] Lord George Murray himself says: "Whatever may be the rules in a regular army (and it is not to be supposed I was ignorant of them), our practice had all along been, at critical junctures, that the commanding officers did everything to their knowledge for the best."—Jacobite Memoirs, p. 39; Lord George Murray's letter to Hamilton of Bangour in Home's Hist., vol. iii. p. 353.

not, and had never intended to, lead his men, and as in the darkness no man, more especially one on foot, could have been either seen or heard, the speech must be reckoned among the many fables which were appropriately manufactured for the purpose of creating personal interest in the Stuart cause. In the same category may be placed the less important but oft-quoted tale of the imaginative Highland officer, a Macdonald, whose narrative in the Lockhart Papers describes Charles as giving his final order to his chief Clanranald and the Duke of Perth, and as saying to himself in Gaelic, "Gres-ort! gres-ort!" that is, "Make haste! make haste!"

When Cope had posted the two squadrons of Hamilton's dragoons on his left, it became sufficiently light for him to observe that the rebels were advancing, and that his flank would be turned by their more extended line. He therefore sent one of his aides-de-camp to Colonel Whiteford, directing him to despatch two guns to the left, for the purpose of checking the outflanking movement. But this order could not be complied with. The artillery-drivers, who were merely hired countrymen, had already gone off with their horses, and their example was followed by the six man-of-war gunners, and then by the four old Scots soldiers attached to the ordnance. Colonel Whiteford was thereby left quite alone to manage the six guns. Old Master Gunner Griffith, who was similarly deserted, was compelled, unassisted, to work six mortars with their "damnified" fuzes, which at best were useless weapons on a battle-field. To make good the want of guns on the left, one of the cavalry squadrons was moved farther down the slope.

Some little delay must have occurred before Whiteford fired the first shot, as his runaway helpers had carried with them the powder-flasks, and he must have had to cut open a cartridge for priming-powder. He says, "On my firing the cannon, the first line opened in the centre" (he was naturally regarding with most attention those nearest his guns), "formed a column to the left, and advanced on me with a swiftness not to be conceived." In fact some five masses of clans were thus formed, headed in each case by the chiefs and their immediate relatives with their best armed followers.[1] Lord George Murray, Lochiel, and Stewart of Ardshiel gallantly led the column on their left, which inclined from the direct line in order to close the dangerous open space between it and the marsh. On observing this oblique advance upon his guns, Cope returned to the right along his front. He calculated the most forward attacking mass to be about 600 in

[1] Cope's Trial, pp. 140, 49, 41.

strength, having a front of at least twenty men and a depth of thirty ranks. Whiteford aimed and discharged his cannon as quickly as possible, but he could only accomplish five rounds in all. Some of them took effect, and caused confusion (Lord Loudon calls it "a great shake") among the Highlanders. On noticing this the royal troops huzzaed; but the clansmen gave cheer for cheer, and immediately getting into order, charged at a run directly in face of the cannon, and continued to fire from their muskets in an irregular manner as they approached; "whilst," Lord Loudon observes, "the other bodies moved slowly till they should see whether they" (the attacking force) "would take effect or not."

As the enemy came on, the artillery guard, instead of standing firm on the right of the guns and delivering their fire, which would have told with fatal effect on the mass before them, left their ground and crowded in confusion behind the ordnance, so as to come within a few yards of Gardiner's squadron, in front of which were the Colonel and Brigadier Fowke.[1] A like unsteadiness was at the same time developed in the squadron itself. Captain Singleton, the major of brigade, states: "As the rebel column, which attacked, was popping and firing, the squadron thereupon began

[1] Cope's Trial, pp. 73, 79.

to be a little shy; which the brigadier observing, called out to them aloud, 'What do you mean, gentlemen, by reining back your horses? Advance to your ground. Have you anything to fear? We shall cut them to pieces in a moment.'" At the same time Fowke ordered Gardiner to incline his squadron nearer to Whitney's on his left; and being anxious to clear the artillery guard out of the way, and replace it on its important position, he called out to Captain Singleton, "I'll go to the right of these people, you go to their left." Both officers strenuously, but with little success, endeavoured to restore order. They managed to "form a front rank, which in great confusion gave a straggling fire, and in a moment fell back with the rest of their body and took to flight; when," the brigadier states, "turning my head to look for the squadron, most of them had in like manner took to flight."

At the moment when the short-lasting confusion or "shake" among the Camerons took place, Colonel Whiteford called out to Colonel Whitney, "Now is your time to attack them"; and Lord Loudon states that he simultaneously conveyed orders to the latter officer "to march his squadron out of the line, in order to attack the Highlanders in flank before they came up to the cannon."[1] At this crisis Cope seemed certain of

[1] Cope's Trial, pp. 49, 411, 40.

victory. From the distance of the second rebel column the cavalry had no danger in their front. The flank of the advancing mass was at their mercy, being totally unprotected. All that the royal horsemen had to do was to charge heartily into it, as the Duke of Argyll's dragoons had done at Sheriffmuir in the previous Rebellion. Formed as they were in a mass, the Highlanders could not have used with freedom either their muskets or swords, and had the foremost column been scattered, the same fate would have befallen the other bodies, if they had ventured in succession to continue the attack.

Colonel Lascelles states that on the squadron moving to the front, " I attempted to wheel some platoons " (in the direction of the enemy) "to assist the dragoons in their charge, and to cover the right of the foot, which I was obliged to stop immediately, as some of the files of the platoons on the right were crouching and creeping gently backwards, with their arms recovered; which was occasioned by continued irregular fire over their heads; which I soon put to rights by my example and reproaches, and kept them firm as long as the fire lasted." Unaware of this infantry failure in duty, Colonel Whitney, to use the words of Lord Loudon, "marched out and wheeled his squadron, and got within pistol-shot of their flank; when, on four or five shot coming from the flank of the Highlanders, the men stopped and could not be got along any further, notwithstanding all the colonel and other officers" (and, it may be added, Lord Loudon) "could do, and immediately the rear rank began to run away, and the rest followed in tens and twenties." Whitney, who had led his men very gallantly, received a shot which shattered his sword-arm. No mention is made, either in the Jacobite narratives or in the clear statements at Cope's trial, of the Highlanders having even paused in their onset to avert the imminent danger which for a few minutes threatened them with overthrow. They ran straight upon the line of mortars and guns, unopposed except by the two solitary officers, Colonel Whiteford and Master Gunner Griffith. Stewart of Invernahyle, according to the graphic story of Sir Walter Scott, "was one of the foremost in the charge, and observing an officer of the king's forces who, scorning to join the flight of all around, remained with his sword in his hand, as if determined to the very last to defend the post assigned to him, the Highland gentleman commanded him to surrender, and received for reply a thrust, which he caught in his target. The officer was now defenceless, and the battle-axe of a gigantic Highlander (the miller of Invernahyle's mill) was uplifted to dash his brains out, when Stewart with difficulty prevailed on him to yield."[1] Master Gunner Griffith was also taken prisoner, both he and his commander having received wounds.

The formation of the attacking column was broken by passing through the ordnance and over the artillery guard. Colonel Gardiner then received orders to charge the now confused mass of assailants; but that unfortunate officer, on looking towards his men, saw them again reining back their horses and turning to fly.[2] He desired his adjutant, Cornet Ker, to ride and stop them. At the same moment, however, he received two gunshot wounds on his right side, and fell from his horse, which got free. Ker states there was no other horse near on which to remount him, and instantly afterwards the rebels came on and cut him over the head. In Sir John's original narrative he mentions that "Colonel Gardiner about this time received his mortal wound, and fell from his horse." But in the main proceedings of the trial this fact is omitted, and the details of the occurrence were only elicited from Cornet Ker by an accidental circumstance. The court, it may be surmised, had directions to abstain from all avoidable allusion to the Colonel, who had many powerful friends, and who had already become a popular

[1] Introduction to 'Waverley,' p. 98, edition of 1829.
[2] Cope's Trial, pp. 41, 55, 81, 96.

hero. The Rev. Dr Doddridge had published his Life, and in it had given too willing credence to the impossible tales, which have ever since been regarded as historical facts, of a soldier named Foster. This narrator had stated that after Gardiner had received one bullet in his left breast and another in his thigh, he had led his Colonel's horse and had in vain tried to persuade him to retreat; but that the Colonel fought on, and that "some of the enemy fell by him," particularly one man who had made a treacherous visit to him a few days before; and that he afterwards took command of a party of foot, who were still fighting bravely, though deserted by their own officers; and that at last he was wounded with a scythe and dragged off his horse by Highlanders, yet that he still had strength to wave his hat and address an order directing the retirement of "his faithful attendant," whose "eye and heart," by his own account, "were always upon his honoured master during the whole time."

The example in flight given by the two squadrons on the right was promptly followed by those in the reserve and on the left flank, who had not received even a semblance of an attack on which to found an excuse for their conduct. "All of them went off so much at the same instant that it is difficult to say which ran first."[1] Captain Clark, who commanded the left squadron of the reserve, states in his evidence that when he first "saw the dragoons in motion, he imagined they were in pursuit of an enemy, but he was quickly undeceived. He called to his own squadron to stand fast and let the crowd pass, and they, the squadron, would be able to ride down the rebels; but this squadron immediately quitted their officers and fled." Brigadier Fowke, with Major Singleton, vainly trying to induce the artillery guard to make a stand, remained in their front until the rebels were within fifteen yards, and then followed the dragoons in their flight towards Lord Grange's park walls, which were a little more than half a mile in rear, in hopes of recalling them to their duty. At about half that distance some thirty of them made a short halt. The Highlanders made a corresponding pause, and the brigadier, placing himself at the head of the horsemen, called out, "Now, lads, take your revenge!" But, as Major Singleton states, "as the rebel column approached pretty near, and gave a fire, away the dragoons all ran, ducking their heads at every pop." Thus left alone, and despairing of getting any fight out of the cavalry, Fowke galloped past the Highlanders near him towards where the right of the foot had stood, as he heard firing in that direction,

[1] Cope's Trial, pp. 41, 80, 73, 78.

and thought he might be of some use to his General. Already, however, all thought of resistance was practically over on the part of this last branch of the royal army.

The second and third attacking columns from the Prince's first line were composed of the Macgregors, commanded by the traitor Major James Macgregor, son of Rob Roy, and of the Duke of Perth's regiment. It has been stated that there was a considerable space of open ground between the united column of Stewarts and Camerons and these bodies, which was attributed by the royal officers to the latter lagging behind for the purpose of seeing how it fared with the first mass before delivering their charge. These surmises are confirmed by Chambers, who, quoting from an original Jacobite manuscript, states that the Perthshire men "stood stock-still like oxen"; but the historian remarks that the Macgregors "at least evinced all the ardour and bravery so generally displayed that day by their countrymen."[1] This may be doubted: the author's only authority is Chevalier Johnstone, one of Lord George Murray's aides-de-camp, who narrates that their major fell pierced with no fewer than five bullets, two of which went quite through his body, and that when prostrate on the field he called out to his clansmen, "Look ye, my lads, I'm

[1] Chambers's Hist., p. 129.

not dead; by God, I shall see if any of you does not do his duty!" This address, Chambers thinks, may have contributed to decide the fate of the day. As a matter of fact, men just after being grievously riddled are not usually fit to make speeches, and charging soldiers give no time to be sworn at and threatened. The battle was otherwise decided. It is, however, obvious that had Whitney's squadron ridden down the left rebel column, Gardiner's squadron, aided by an infantry fire in front, would have been able to dispose of the Macgregors, whose unprotected left flank invited attack.

The breaking up of the royal infantry line began from the right, where Colonel Lascelles, acting as brigadier, had, after dismounting, posted himself. He states: "Upon the dragoons going off, the left column of the rebels broke, and pursued them sword in hand as fast as they could run, except about 150 of the rear, who halted upon the right of the artillery, and near upon a line with it, till the other two columns of the rebels began to fire upon the front, when they moved off rapidly with a seeming design to attack our right flank, which I intended to guard against by wheeling three platoons that were not engaged."[1] It has been mentioned that shortly before he had attempted the same manœuvre, but had been obliged to desist on

[1] Cope's Trial, pp. 66, 69.

account of the unsteadiness of the soldiers. On this occasion also he failed by his men running away altogether. He says that "in moving fast to direct the wheeling, he had the misfortune to fall, and though he rose as quick as possible, he found an officer of the rebels with sixteen men just upon him, who told him he was his prisoner, and directed him to give up his arms to a man he, the officer, pointed at, which he was obliged to submit to." The Highlanders had only about 160 yards to pass over between the right of the artillery and that of the out-guards; yet it was difficult to understand how he had not time to wheel the men, to fall, and to rise again, before the enemy were upon him. This, however, is explained by the note on the incident made by the officer of Lee's regiment, whose remarks upon his copy of Cope's Trial have been already spoken of. This note is as follows: "Colonel Lascelles intended to cover the right flank by ordering them to wheel to the left"—*i.e.*, inwards with their backs to the rebels. "Upon perceiving his mistake he ordered them to fall back again, which put them into confusion, and the rebels firing, they went off." There are few old soldiers who have not seen similar blunders accidentally made, even by usually clear-headed men, on ordinary parades. This mistake is stated with apparent truth to have occurred at the critical moment of the action. Its consequences were irretrievable and fatal. The last hope of victory for the royal army was lost. The artillery had been captured. The cavalry had fled. One flank was now rolled up without the possibility of effectual resistance, and the other had been left bare by the flight of the dragoons. At the same time there were heard in the rear the shouts and firing of the Highlanders, who had pursued the cavalry.

On perceiving the success of their left, the centre rebel columns, as well as the Macdonalds on their right, who had never paused in their onset, but had had a longer distance to move over, advanced with confidence and rapidity. They were followed at an interval of some 200 yards by their second line, which would have overlapped the royal right had it stood its ground. The Highlanders as they approached gave a dropping irregular fire at such a distance as to cause little execution. The fire delivered by the king's troops must have been even less effective. The Earl of Home says, "The foot could with difficulty be prevailed upon to give one fire, and that a bad one; and when that was over, broke." Lord Loudon calls it "an irregular fire by dropping shots"; and Lord Drummore, who styles himself "a most sensibly interested spectator," described it as "infamous, puff, puff, and no platoon."

Then, as Colonel Whiteford testified, "all ran shamefully without making the slightest resistance." Major Talbot, who was on the left, states that "he saw the breaking up of the foot come on regularly, as it were by platoons, from the right to the left. He and the rest of the officers did everything in their power to stop the men from running away, but to no purpose." It was first tried to replace them on their original ground, and then, for their own safety, to form them into a body—but in vain. They could not even be got to reload their muskets. They fled while still at distant musket-range from the enemy, and not one bayonet was stained with blood. Cope himself, always between the soldiers and their foes, did all that man could do to rally them. Nine officers, who had been stationed on that morning in different parts of the line, were examined at the General's trial, especially as to his personal conduct. They, with other witnesses, to a man bore testimony to his gallant behaviour. Lord Loudon says he was everywhere. Two officers mention the words he used to their own soldiers. Captain Pointz of Guise's regiment states that he called out to them, "For shame, gentlemen! behave like Britons; give them another fire and you'll make them run." Another, Lieutenant Greenwell of Murray's, recollected his ordering his men to halt and saying, "For shame, gentlemen! don't let us be beat by such a set of banditti." But, notwithstanding all that Sir John and the rest of the officers could do, the troops dispersed, and very soon the more light-footed Highlanders were mingled with them, maiming and slaughtering at their wild discretion.

Many of the foregoing details are in direct variance with the histories of Scott, Chambers, and Lord Mahon, which are for the most part repetitions of the narratives of the Jacobites and of Dr Doddridge. The tales of the Highlanders reverentially uncovering their heads and uttering a short prayer before the action began; of pipers blowing the signal for the general advance; of the artillery playing furiously on their columns on the left and raking their right wing; of their war-cries rising into terrible yells; of their pouring a heavy rolling fire into, and waving their plaids before, the dragoons when being led in a gallant charge by Colonel Gardiner; of their leaders, Lochiel on the left and Clanranald on the right, at the same time penetrating Cope's thin red line; of their centre being received by a steady well-directed fire from the king's foot, who stood fighting till no longer able to withstand the fury of the onset; of the general throwing away of their muskets and parrying the thrusts of the soldiers' bayonets with their targets, and slaying their opponents with their broadswords,—these tales are originally all carefully fabricated fictions. Even Murray of Broughton states that opposite the Prince's right wing "the foot likewise fired too soon, and almost all turned their backs before the Highlanders could engage them with their swords."[1] That there was at first a space between the flying infantry and their pursuers is casually proved by the adventures of Brigadier Fowke, who has been mentioned as returning towards the original position of the infantry. He had ridden through some of the fugitives, and was approaching a clump of men who were firing as they advanced, when Captain Wedderburn, a volunteer, called out to him, "Sir, these are the enemy before you."[2] The brigadier then rode to the left and met Captain Christie of Murray's regiment, who describes the circumstances as follows: "When the panic seized our line of foot, and made them run away a minute or two afterwards, we were deserted by the dragoons. I ran with the crowd at first for about 300 yards towards Mr Erskine's" (Lord Grange) "inclosures, the rebels pursuing us close. I then ran out of the crowd towards the sea. I met an officer's servant, who had continued in the left on our rear, with his master's horse, which I mounted. . . .

[1] Murray of Broughton's Narrative, p. 20.
[2] Cope's Trial, pp. 73, 78, 80.

Just as I got on horseback I saw General Fowke, with his sword drawn, galloping out of the crowd running away. He asked me which way we had better take to avoid being made prisoners. . . . I told him our best way was to ride to the seaside and make our way by the coast road eastwards. We did so, and the few of the stragglers of the enemy who remained on the field suffered us to go off unmolested. We stayed some time at Beltonford, and got to Berwick that night," a distance of thirty-eight miles. The escape of Colonel Lascelles to Berwick on the same day may here be mentioned. Shortly after being captured and disarmed, his guard, unable to resist the temptation of going after the red-coats, left him alone and free. Seeing a clear space over the ground in his front which had been recently crossed by the rebel left column, he walked straight over it, with Highlanders on his right and left, but all too intent on joining in the general pursuit to regard a solitary man. He thus unharmed reached Seton, which he could not have succeeded in doing if the field had been at all thickly strewn with dead and wounded men, who would probably have had with them a few attendants. At Seton he procured a horse and rode off.

All the endeavours of Cope and his officers to rally the infantry having utterly failed, he galloped to where he observed that many of the cavalry, instead of escaping by the narrow roads or defiles on the south-west of the battle-field, had massed against Lord Grange's park wall. The day before this wall had been for the most part reduced in height to enable infantry to fire over it, but it was still too high for horsemen to surmount. Lord Loudon describes the subsequent occurrences as follows: "The General rode up to them, in hopes there to make a stand, but to no effect; for they stood with their croups to the enemy, and all the world could not turn them, though the Highlanders were continually firing at them as they came running on. In this situation there was nothing left but to carry them through the defile" (between Lord Grange's and Colonel Gardiner's park walls), "to form behind the village" (of Preston), "which was accordingly done. The Earl of Home stood in the road, with his pistol in his hand, to turn them into the field, where there were about three squadrons" (Cope says 450 men) "gathered. By the time that one was formed, and the others gathered into two bodies, a body of Highlanders presented themselves at the" (west) "end of the lane" (or defile). "On seeing the dragoons formed, they halted; on which it was proposed to attack them with the squadron that was formed, seeing they stood in awe. But they" (the dragoons) "could not be brought to move one foot."[1] By this time the Highlanders had completely broken from any military formation in the pursuit, slaughter, capture, and pillage of the infantry, and had these 450 horsemen plucked up sufficient courage to return to the field, they might have ridden over it at will, slaying the slayers, and very probably they might have killed or captured the Prince himself. Under existing circumstances, however, Sir John, again to quote the words of the adjutant-general, "thought it necessary to move them still further off; and as soon as the march began, the officers fell into rear, as usual in retreats; but the men immediately began to gallop off; and it was found there was no other way of getting them to make a decent retreat but by keeping at their head, in order to keep them back. They were formed three different times towards the enemy to make the retreat look as decent as possible; after which Sir John consulted with his principal officers that were along with him, which way he ought to move. It was agreed on by all that it was improper for him to go to Edinburgh with so small a force, when it was evident he could not defend it against the rebels; and the only thing he had left was to get to Berwick, to join the Dutch who were expected there." Accordingly the dragoons were

[1] Cope's Trial, pp. 140, 43.

marched southwards across the Lammermuirs to Lauder, where they made a short halt for refreshment, and where Cope wrote to Lord Tweeddale a simple and true despatch, fully acknowledging his total defeat. In it he says: "I have been unfortunate, which will certainly give a handle to my enemies to cast blame upon me. I cannot reproach myself. The manner in which the enemy came on, which was quicker than can be described (of which the men had been long warned), possibly was the cause of our men taking a most destructive panic."[1] The troops then resumed their march, and rested for the night at Coldstream and Cornhill. Old Sir John Clerk of Penicuik, a Baron of Exchequer, was at this time flying before the rebels into temporary exile. His 'Autobiography' has been recently published, and in it there is the following entry: "The regiments of dragoons went off" (from the battle) "pretty entire. One of them came that night to Cannal" (Cornhill, near Coldstream), "where my wife and I chanced to be, and the other to Coldstream, so that they made a march that day of above thirty-five miles. . . . As many of the officers came to lodge under us in the same house, we thought hell had broken loose, for I never heard such oaths and imprecations, branding each other with cowardice and

[1] Cope's Trial, p. 193.

neglect of duty."[1] On the following day they reached Berwick.

To return to the field of battle. Lord George Murray states that "we on the left pursued to the walls and lane near Colonel Gardiner's house. Some of them" (the foot) "were rallying behind us, but when they saw our second line coming up, they then made the best of their way. A lieutenant-colonel" (Halkett of Lee's regiment) "with five other officers and about fourteen men of the enemy got over the ditch" (which ran along the south margin of the field) "and fired at us. I got before a hundred of our men, who had their guns presented to fire upon them, and at my desire they kept up" (reserved) "their fire, so that those officers and soldiers surrendered themselves prisoners; and nothing gave me more pleasure that day than having it so immediately in my power to save those men, as well as several others. Many prisoners were taken by Lochiel's people in the heat of action." (His silence regarding like conduct on the part of other clansmen is ominous.) "A good many dragoons passed us a little after, but most of them were dismounted"—*i.e.*, either they or their horses were shot —"before they reached the lane. Lochiel kept his men very well together, and they were the first who

[1] Memoirs of Sir J. Clerk, p. 185.

rallied in a body. I was told that a number of the enemy were gathering in a body near Tranent, and I perceived a good many people on the height. I immediately marched, with Lochiel and his regiment, back to the narrow causeway" (on which was the waggon-way) "that led up to Tranent; but when I was half-way up, we found those we had taken for enemies were mostly servants belonging to our army, and some country-people. I got intelligence at the same time that a number of the enemy were at Cockenny" (Cockenzie). "I immediately made the rear the front of Lochiel's men"—*i.e.*, made all face to the right about—"and marched straight to Cockenny, leaving our prisoners with a guard. This place was about a mile distant. There were about 300 of the enemy there, above the half of them being their Highlanders. As they were within walls, they thought of defending themselves."[1] These Highlanders consisted of two companies of the Black Watch under Sir Patrick Murray of Auchtertyre, and three very weak companies of Lord Loudon's regiment, who had been sent the evening before to relieve the infantry baggage-guard at Cockenzie. As their strength could not have come up to 200 men, Lord George's numbers must have been made up of officers' servants and other

[1] Jacobite Memoirs, p. 41.

followers, with probably a few fugitives from the battlefield. Murray of Broughton writes that Captain Basil Cochran of Lee's regiment, one of the prisoners, was sent "to tell them that if they would immediately surrender as prisoners of war, they should be used as such; if not, they would be immediately attacked, and no quarter given, upon which they readily gave up their arms." "The whole baggage of the army was taken, and amongst the rest the military chest, hid under a staircase in Cockenny House amongst a parcel of old barrels and other limber, where was found between two and three thousand" (pounds), "with the General's papers; the rest of the money, as is alleged, having been conveyed by sea on board a man-of-war in the Roads."[1] The Whig writer, Henderson, whose very popular History was dedicated to the Prince of Wales, and who never lost an opportunity of lashing at Cope, says that there were £4000 in the chest, and that Sir John himself had taken the precaution of placing a portion of his gold on board the Fox frigate before he left Dunbar. He adds that this "was the only prudent step he took during this fatal and inglorious campaign."[2]

[1] Murray of Broughton, pp. 203, 209.
[2] Henderson's Hist., p. 87; Lyon in Mourning, vol. i. p. 292.

CHAPTER IX.

THE victory of Prince Charles was most complete. Of the infantry not above 200 escaped. Of these 105 were mustered in Edinburgh Castle on the following Monday, and 70 made their way back to Berwick. The account issued from headquarters says that 500 of the royal army were killed and 1400 made prisoners, of whom 900 were wounded.[1] Some of the prisoners, doubtless, were camp-followers. By other accounts the wounds in many cases were of a hideous description. Sir Walter Scott, without stating his authority, reduces the number of the slain to 400, and remarks that "the Highlanders gave little quarter in the first moments of excitation, though those did not last long." This statement is not borne out by the testimony of eyewitnesses. According to Johnstone, Lord George Murray's aide-

[1] Home's Hist., vol. iii., note, p. 95; Gentleman's Magazine, October 1745, p. 517.

de-camp, who happened during the charge to be on duty with the Prince, "the Highlanders made a terrible slaughter of the enemy, particularly at the spot where the road begins to run between the two inclosures, as it was soon stopped up by the fugitives; as also along the walls of the inclosures, where they killed, without trouble, those who attempted to climb them." [1] And Carlyle mentions that little more than fifteen minutes after the firing of the first gun he was standing on "a mount" at the corner of his father's manse garden, nearly a mile from the battle-field, and saw "the whole prospect filled with runaways, and Highlanders pursuing them. Many had their coats turned as prisoners, but were still trying to reach the town in hopes of escaping. The Highlanders, when they could not overtake them, fired at them, and I saw two fall in the glebe." The rules of war, however, permit prisoners trying to escape to be freely shot. After the action was over, one young savage was formally presented to the Prince on account of his having cut down fourteen flying soldiers with his sword; and Charles is stated to have specially noticed and regaled a party of Macgregors who had been conspicuous in the pursuit and slaughter. The historian

---

[1] Tales of a Grandfather, vol. iii. p. 34; Johnstone's Memoirs, p. 28; Carlyle's Autobiography, p. 142.

Henderson wrote that at this time he himself came upon the field, and "saw the young Chevalier, who, by the advice of Perth, had sent to Edinburgh for surgeons: his horse stood near him, with his armour of tin (?), which resembled a woman's stays, affixed to the saddle; he was on foot, clad as an ordinary captain in a coarse plaid and large blue bonnet, a scarlet waistcoat with a narrow plain gold-lace about it, his boots and knees were much dirtied" (the effect of having fallen into a ditch); "he was exceedingly merry, and twice said, 'My Highlanders have lost their plaids'; at which he laughed very heartily, being no way affected when speaking of the dead and wounded. Nor would his jollity have been interrupted, if he had not looked upon seven standards that had been taken from the dragoons; on which he said in French (a language he frequently spoke in), 'We have missed some of them.' After this he refreshed himself, and with the utmost composure ate a piece of cold beef and drank a glass of wine amidst the deep and piercing groans of the poor men, who had been wounded in seven or eight places, and had fallen a sacrifice to his ambition. Thereafter he rode through Preston to Pinkie House (a seat, near Musselburgh, belonging to the Marquis of Tweeddale), leaving the bulk of the wounded upon the field till next day, who were brought upon carts into Edinburgh."[1] The explanation of the Prince's mirth appears to be that in 1745 the kilt separate from the plaid was not part of the Highland costume. One end of the plaid, under which was worn a shirt, was wrapped round the waist, and the remainder of it was thrown over the shoulder, forming a combination garment such as is still worn, but of cooler material, in many oriental countries. When speed was required it was laid aside. Dugald Graham, describing the Highlanders at the battle of Falkirk, says—

> "Their plaids in heaps were left behind,
> Light to run if need they find."

It was, apparently, the sight of his men only in their shirts that called forth princely merriment. Lord George Murray, however, states that his Royal Highness "caused take the same care of their wounded as of his own." And Murray of Broughton asserts that "the Chevalier gave orders to have the wounded dressed and carriages provided to take them off the field, which was executed by his surgeons, with all the care and expedition imaginable, to the great loss of the wounded of his own army, who from being neglected till most of the troops were taken care of,

[1] Chambers's Hist., p. 133; Henderson's Hist., p. 88.

their wounds festered, being all gunshot and mostly in the legs and thighs. He breakfasted on the field, but not amongst the dead and within hearing of the groans of the wounded, as has been falsely asserted by a little ignorant *schoolmaster*" (Henderson), "who has pretended to write the history of an affair of which he could not judge."[1] But in the middle of a field so limited in extent and so plentifully strewn with fallen soldiers, it would have been hard to escape from sights and sounds which for the time destroy the appetite and mirth of most men. These and similar charges of callousness probably caused the insertion of humane and noble sentiments regarding the wounded sufferers in a long letter stated to have been written by Charles to his father on the very day of the battle. This production appears to have been widely circulated, as copies were in the possession of Bishop Forbes and others. Chambers published it in full in the first editions of his History, having probably copied it from the Bishop's manuscript, then in his hands. Ewald publishes it in his Life of Prince Charles as a true State document ("No. 244, State Papers, Domestic: never before published"). It bears intrinsic evidence of being a fabrication, apparently by the same unscrupulous

---

[1] Jacobite Memoirs, p. 42; Murray of Broughton's Narrative, p. 21.

hand which made up another lengthy letter in the same style, pretended to have been written by the Prince on the eve of his leaving Perth. Lord Mahon says of it, "I am surprised that Mr Chambers should have been imposed upon by a clumsy forgery."[1] Charles's real and very short letter about the action was not written till 7th October. It contains no lofty thoughts, but speaks of Cope's horse having escaped "like rabbits, one by one," and of his own army as having "had a fine plunder."

Shortly after the firing had ceased, there rode on to the field an intimate friend of Colonel Gardiner, Mr Andrew Wight, who resided at Ormiston, a village about three miles distant. To his care the Colonel had on the previous day consigned his two eldest daughters, who up to that time had continued to live at Bankton. Anxious to know the result of the fighting, Mr Wight left his house early in the morning of the 21st, and before he reached the scene met some runaway dragoons, but could not learn from them their Colonel's fate. On reaching the field he was told that his friend had been slain, and, to use the words of a well-informed writer, "being acquainted with the

---

[1] Lyon in Mourning, vol. i. p. 211; Ewald's Life of Prince Charles, p. 128; Mahon's The '45, pp. 58, 154.

Duke of Perth,[1] he went forward and asked permission to search for and remove the body. The Duke answered that as the officers were all coming up to wish the Prince joy of the victory, if he could wait a little he would ask from the Prince the permission wanted. He accordingly came aside and granted the request, at the same time pointed out near to the spot where Colonel Gardiner fell. Mr Wight proceeded to the spot, and found the Colonel mortally wounded, and almost stripped, but still alive, though he never spoke again. He bought a Highlander's plaid, and had him wrapped in it, and carried to the manse of Tranent (then occupied by the Rev. Charles Cunningham, brother-in-law to Mr Wight), where he died" next day.[2] The manse was as near the spot where the unfortunate officer fell as his own residence, which was already being utilised as a hospital, principally for the Highland wounded. In the first sermon which he preached afterwards at Ormiston, the parish minister indignantly complained that Gardiner's residence should have thus been desecrated and exposed to partial plunder; but, as a matter of fact, it had been used as a garrisoned military post by

[1] The Duke of Perth, Colonel Gardiner, and Mr Wight were all members of the Ormiston Agricultural Society, which had been instituted by John Cockburn of Ormiston in 1736 (Farmer's Magazine, No. 18, quoted in the 'Lamp of Lothian,' p. 272).

[2] Edinburgh Courant, September 1828.

Cope till just before the action, and, with the exception of Lord Grange's, it was the nearest gentleman's mansion to where the wounded lay.[1] It is creditable to the discipline, or perhaps to the simplicity, of the rebels that they were so much pleased with the "fine plunder" they had obtained from the dead, the captives, and the baggage of the enemy, that little annoyance was given to other residents in the vicinity.

The Jacobite official account gave their casualties on the field as amounting to 4 officers and about 30 men killed, and 1 officer and about 70 or 80 men wounded. All historians have accepted these numbers as accurate. But this account is in some other details fabulous, and these numbers are incredible, when consideration is given to the slight resistance made by the royal troops on their extreme right only; to the slight loss caused by the fire of the unmanned guns; to the single, distant, and unsteady musketry discharge; and to neither cavalry sword nor infantry bayonet having been stained by foeman's blood. It was politic and necessary to magnify their losses, so as to avoid shocking the national feelings by the contrast with the undeniable slaughter of Cope's men, and in order that they might harmonise to a certain extent with the tales of storming the royal artillery; of firing furiously; of the

[1] Scots Magazine, p. 467, 1745.

very regular volleys from 3000 or 4000 infantry; of their reserving their own musketry charge till the wadding of their cartridges set fire to the whiskers of the soldiers; and of a final desperate hand-to-hand contest between the bayonets of the foot and the broadsword and targets of the Highlanders. There seems, however, to have been a sort of mystery on the subject in the minds of the earlier writers, as the dead were not very visible; and the popular story that they had concealed their losses is reflected in the lines of Dugald Graham, whose rhyming history had a very large circulation. He says—

> "Yet of their loss they let not ken,
> For by the shot fell not a few,
> And many with bay'nots pierced through."[1]

The writer of the Jacobite little history styled 'The Wanderer' accounts for the alleged number of the slain by saying that, though not above a dozen were killed on the field, most of the wounded died that night. Ray in his History writes, "The rebels encircled their dead, and buried them with all expedition to conceal their number."[2] The author of 'The Wanderer,' however, gives some valuable extracts from a French

---

[1] D. Graham, 8th edition, p. 23.
[2] The Wanderer, pp. 31, 53 et seq.; Ray's Compleat History, p. 40; Carlyle's Autobiography, p. 146.

manuscript, which, he says, accident threw in his way. It was the journal of a gentleman with the Marquis of Tullibardine, who had assumed the Atholl dukedom and estates, and whom the Prince had left in command of the country to the north of the Forth. The journalist records that on the 20th September "le Prince envoyait un exprès au Duc, qu'il étoit arrivé à Edimbourg, capital d'Ecosse, est que la ville étoit illuminée par tout, sinon le fort qui n'étoit pas rendu." And again on "le 3 [octobre] *N.S.*"—22nd September, *O. S.*—"le Duc [Atholl] a reçu une lettre du Prince, qu'il avait été victorieux d'une bataille : qu'il y avait cinq cents de tuéz et trois brigades de prisonniers. Le Prince a perdu environ une douzaine de soldats." This was probably the true estimate of rebel loss, and tallies with the recorded statement of the Duke of Perth's armour-bearer, who a few hours after the fray boasted to young Carlyle of the certainty of their future success, "as the Almighty had blessed them with an almost bloodless victory."

Some interesting episodes of the later events of the day are given in the narratives of Carlyle and Lord George Murray. The father of the former became uneasy about the safety of his son, who had been so keen a volunteer. Both the Carlyles, therefore, mounted their horses and endeavoured to escape eastwards by Cockenzie; but just beyond that place they came upon Highlanders rather freely shooting down baggage-cart drivers, who were also trying to get beyond the clutches of the rebels. This rough procedure daunted the old minister, and both returned to Prestonpans, to which place by this time some twenty-three badly wounded and hacked officers of the royal army had been carried, and had, under the personal care of the Duke of Perth, been placed in the house of Mr Cheape, the local collector of customs.[1] Carlyle then details taking off his boots and putting on shoes, so as to give himself the general appearance of a person who had not been abroad, and then offering his services to Surgeons Cunningham (afterwards the most distinguished surgeon in Dublin) and Trotter of the dragoons, who had surrendered in order to attend upon the wounded. His first case was that of a very handsome young officer, Captain Blake of Murray's regiment, who was lying in an easy-chair in a faint, and seemingly dying. Beside him on a chest of drawers lay a piece of his skull, about two fingers' breadth and an inch and a half long. Carlyle remarked, "This gentleman must die." "No," said Cunningham; "the brain is not affected, nor any vital part, and could I but get my instruments, there would

[1] Carlyle's Autobiography, p. 144.

be no fear of him." Carlyle was accordingly despatched with an escort, willingly provided by the rebel Captain Stewart (described as being grave, good-looking, and of polished manners), for the purpose of trying to find a medicine-chest among the captured baggage at Cockenzie. On their way they met a couple of grooms leading four blood-horses. The leader of the escort promptly darted at the foremost, and presenting his pistol, demanded, "Who are you, sir? and where are you going?" An answer was humbly given with uncovered head, "I am Sir John Cope's coachman, and I am seeking my master"; to which the Highlander replied, "You'll not find him here, sir, but you and your man and your horses are my prisoners." On reaching Cockenzie, Carlyle (who in after-years is called by Sir Walter Scott "a shrewd, clever old carle") had an opportunity of seeing a fair sample of the victorious army.[1] All were in good humour, for successful looting has a soothing effect on civilised as well as on savage breasts. The men, he thought, were of low stature, dirty, and of contemptible appearance; but the officers were gentlemanlike, and very civil to him in trying to find a medicine-chest. The search was unsuccessful, but instruments were

[1] Carlyle's Autobiography, p. 567; Lockhart's Life of Scott, vol. iv. p. 1461.

elsewhere procured; and it is satisfactory to know that fifty-five years afterwards Carlyle and Captain Blake accidentally met in London and "uncorked a bottle of wine together."

On his way back to Prestonpans Carlyle saw walking on the sea-shore all the officers who had been taken prisoners, excepting those who had been very grievously wounded. "Every aspect bore in it shame, dejection, and despair. They were deeply mortified at what had happened, and doubtful whether they were to be treated as prisoners of war or as rebels." They were comforted by hearing how kindly the wounded officers had been treated, and by the young man's venturing to assert his confidence that the other prisoners would be treated with similar humanity. His belief was not belied; for in the evening Lord George Murray, giving the weakest of them the use of his own horses, walked with them to a house allotted for them at Musselburgh. It was found to have in it no furniture of any kind, but Murray bought newly threshed straw for the floors, and regaled them with a tolerable meal from his own stock of cold provisions and liquors, and then sent the most sickly of them to the minister's house, which had been assigned as his own quarters. He was about to leave for the night the prisoners, who had given him their parole not to attempt to escape, when he found that no guard had been detailed to watch over them, and that they were in reasonable apprehension of being insulted and plundered by drunken Highlanders. Lord George, therefore, lay down on the floor with them all night, and next morning, as soon as the Prince had left Pinkie House on his triumphant return to Edinburgh, he had them all removed to that comfortable mansion. It might be tedious to narrate his continued efforts to alleviate the condition of the prisoners and wounded, but it may be mentioned that when the officers were a week afterwards sent to Perthshire, they marched under a protective guard of Murray's own men, and that he specially wrote to his brother, the Marquis of Tullibardine, detailing measures likely to shield them from harm or insult. All this humane care is in sad contrast to the savage treatment to which the Stuart prisoners were subjected as soon as the Hanoverian Government felt confident of victory. In 1749 Lord George was a hopeless exile, and had been basely treated by the Prince, for whose sake he had made such heavy sacrifices. At that time the Scottish poet, Hamilton of Bangour, who had also escaped abroad after joining in the Rebellion, had just received his pardon. Murray, under the signature of De Vallignie, wrote to him the following touching words: " I wish you all happiness and contentment in the Land of Cakes, where, I assure you, my heart is; and though the pleasure of being there be debarred me, yet I promise you it gives me much satisfaction to know that some of my fellow-countrymen who were engaged with us have escaped the jaws of the voracious wolves, though I am apt to believe it was more owing to their oversight than mercy. Be that as it will, I wish from the bottom of my heart that more were in the same condition, and that I were myself the only sufferer, which would make me bear my private loss without a grudge."

The effects, political and moral, of the action at Prestonpans were out of all proportion to the small numbers of the forces which had been engaged in the struggle. Prince Charles at once became master of the whole of Scotland except a few fortresses and certain districts in the North, where the influence of Lord President Forbes was still dominant; and throughout the civilised world he was regarded as a hero in reality, instead of being one of mere fancy or romance. Prospects of effective aid were held out by France, and small supplies of men and money were actually sent without delay. In England a general feeling of alarm superseded the apathy which had hitherto prevailed. The consternation in towns on the route from Edinburgh to London may be learnt from Dr Wesley, who was at Newcastle at the time, and wrote, " The walls are mounted with cannon, and all things prepared for sustaining an assault; but our poor neighbours are busy in removing their goods, and most of the best houses are left without either furniture or inhabitants."[1] King George himself began to realise the serious danger of the insurrection; yet seven days after the battle Horace Walpole wrote, " His Majesty uses his Ministers as ill as possible, and discourages everybody that would risk their lives and fortunes for him."

It is true that the desertion of many Highlanders from his army put it out of the power of the Prince to carry out his original design of availing himself of the road laid open to him for the immediate march towards London; but the grave and unexpected crisis, brought about by a fraction of the Highland clansmen, whom Lord Tweeddale called "the scum of the Camerons and Macdonalds," caused humiliation and anger to the mass of the nation.[2] None could boast of successful effort in resisting the insurrection. Every one felt that somebody must be to blame for the unhappy collapse; but no one dared to name the king as being mainly responsible for the disaster, and for the miseries certain to arise from a continued civil war. An im-

[1] Mahon's The '45, pp. 60, 58.   [2] Home's Hist., vol. iii.

mediate scapegoat was needed, and it seemed to be a relief for all parties to find in Cope a convenient victim. To the ridicule to which his measures had already been exposed were now added attacks on his honesty as a man and on his personal courage as a soldier, till, to use the apt quotation of Sir Walter Scott, he was doomed to remain

> "Sacred to ridicule his whole life long,
> And the sad burden of a merry song."

The story of the savage reception untruly alleged to have been given to Sir John the day after the battle by Lord Mark Ker, commanding at Berwick, may be noticed as an example of the unfair treatment to which he was subjected. Sir Walter Scott's craving to exalt what he terms "the hereditary wit" of a great family in his native Border country may, perhaps, excuse him for repeating as a historical fact the asserted sarcastic welcome of Ker to Cope,—"That he believed he was the first general in Europe who had brought the first tidings of his own defeat."[1] A poet's licence may be allowed to Skirving for his verse on the General's arrival—

> "Now, Johnnie, troth, ye wasna blate
> To come wi' the news o' your ain defeat,
> And leave your men in sic a strait
> Sae early in the morning."

---

[1] Tales of a Grandfather, vol. iii. p. 34.

But the repetition of the story by after-writers—such as Chambers, Lord Mahon, and Ewald — is scarcely pardonable, when the evidence on Cope's trial incidentally, but certainly, proves that the two officers immediately under Cope in the action, Brigadier Fowke and Colonel Lascelles, and at least one other officer, Captain Christie, reached Berwick on the day of the battle, while Sir John, marching *via* Coldstream, did not enter the town till next day.

Cope's arrival at Berwick deprived Lord Mark Ker of his local command. This supersession was disliked by his lordship, who consequently in no good humour withdrew to London.[1] Craigie, the Lord Advocate, who with other Scottish officials had fled to Berwick, mentions, as an instance of Cope's punctilio, that after Lord Mark's departure service-letters arrived addressed to him. They were believed to contain useful information, yet Sir John would not avail himself of them till their seals were broken by other officials present. Lord Drummore, who, as has been mentioned, had been with the king's troops at Prestonpans, appears to have been the first to make him aware of the grave charges now being made against him. In a letter from Alnwick, dated 24th October, Drummore wrote to the General : " Before I left Berwick to attend

---

[1] Omond's Lives of the Lord Advocates.

my friend the Earl of Loudon aboard the Glasgow" (a man-of-war) "at Shields, I observed the dragoons, several of them of Hamilton's and of poor Gardiner's regiments, at first mutter something in their defence, and afterwards they grew a good deal bolder; and in my hearing some of them took the liberty to blame the officers" (it may be presumed that officers of the dragoons were the accusers, and that they were blaming the higher officers of the army), "but I did not hear that any of them had taken the freedom to attack your character in so foul a manner as since I came to this part of the country I find they have. And it does extremely surprise me that, upon no better evidence than theirs, a good many people of sense too should be so credulous as to give credit to some of the stories they affirm as truth. My regard to it, as well as to you, led me to notice several of them in a company where Sir Harry Liddell was, and who did me the honour to ask me to dine with him and some of his friends of this place, to whose satisfaction I had the happiness to clear you of all the imputations thrown upon you." In a postscript he adds: "This country is full of the vilest scandal, which the dragoons, who guarded Mr Lockhart, have had the infamous boldness to utter. They reproach you for want of personal courage, and correspondence close with the Chevalier;

the naming of which things I take to be sufficient refutation of them. So false and malicious are they, that these scandals will soon vanish. Adieu." Lord Drummore's anticipations with regard to the charge of treachery were realised. It died away, as there was not a shadow of proof that Cope had not been thoroughly loyal to the reigning dynasty. But the other accusations have held their ground in history.

Among the loudest to proclaim that the national calamities had been caused principally through Cope's cowardice and incompetence was the merciless General Hawley, who in December was gazetted as his successor in the command of Scotland. It was not to be expected that the luckless Cope could be retained in this appointment. But George II. still gave him some support. He was in attendance at Court when the news arrived of Hawley's disgraceful defeat at Falkirk in January of the following year; and it is recorded — perhaps with a touch of malice — that in the whole assembly the only countenances which retained a serene and pleased expression were those of Cope and the sturdy old king. A letter, however, from Sir John in the ensuing June to his staunch friend Lord President Forbes, shows how keenly he felt his false position. In it he says, "The hardships I have and still do lie under are most cruel."[1] He flatters himself that Forbes and Lord Loudon would try to put his actions in a true light before the Duke of Cumberland, who, with Hawley under him, then held supreme military sway in Scotland, and who had left London deeply prejudiced against him; and he adds: "Being unfortunate in this country is a crime in the mouths of the envious, and of those who are ready to defame a man when fashion is against him. I have the comfort of an honest man, that I neglected no part of my duty, and I cannot reproach myself with anything that ought to reflect on my character. This has enabled me to stand the reproaches of others. . . . I ask pardon; I will have done with the subject. The friendship your lordship honoured me with in Scotland entitles me to claim a continuance of it, since I know not an action of mine which should forfeit it." The reply of Forbes was sympathetic, and regarding his communications with the Duke of Cumberland he wrote: "You have been truly informed about Lord Loudon and your humble servant. We have never varied our style, because truth is stubborn; it will not vary, and those who have a true respect for it dare not attempt to violate it." But the able editor of the Culloden Papers adds, in a note ap-

[1] Culloden Papers, pp. 277, 281.

pended to the letter: "The triumphs of the rebels and the disappointment of the well-affected had equally contributed to throw the unfortunate commander into contempt; and ridicule was kept alive by every art of song and anecdote."

When the country had become somewhat settled after the miserable collapse of Prince Charles's schemes, and of the loudly proclaimed resolves of either conquering or dying in the prosecution of those schemes, and shortly before the impossible young candidate for the British throne had succeeded in escaping from Scotland, Cope's desire for a public inquiry into his conduct was granted by the king. It had also been demanded by the voice of the public, who thirsted for vengeance on the supposed culprit. Had he been found to have been at fault, he would certainly and deservedly have been brought before a court-martial, and would probably have met a fate similar to Admiral Bing's. As soon as Sir John knew that his behaviour was to be examined into, "he acquainted the Secretary of War that he should be glad to have, if possible, every person who had been an eyewitness to any part of his conduct summoned; to which it was answered that it might be inconvenient to his Majesty's service to have some of them, such as Lord Loudon and others, called from the duties they were on. Then

Sir John requested that all such who could be spared might be summoned, and accordingly they were."[1] Truth is indebted for the exact details of the catastrophe at Prestonpans and other important facts to the records of this court, which would probably never have been known had not an anonymous gentleman considered it to be his duty to procure and publish them. He had attended the court as an enemy of Cope—not, however, influenced by personal or political feelings, but by deliberate opinions based upon a careful study of the narratives of the various events as they were alleged to have occurred in the press of the period. His account of the proceedings is as follows:—

"This inquiry was indeed managed with a strictness and solemnity that excluded all suspicion of bias or partiality. The general officers who presided were Field-Marshal George Wade, President, Lieutenant-Generals Charles Lord Cadogan, John Folliot, Charles Duke of Richmond, and John Guise. None of these gentlemen had at any time been so much as suspected of a behaviour the least resembling that charged on Sir John Cope; but were all of them of unblemished honour and distinguished justice, and were competent judges of the matters intrusted to their examination. Every

[1] Cope's Trial, p. 62.

officer who had marched with the army from Stirling, except a few whose services could not be dispensed with, and whose letters therefore were permitted to be read, and the volunteers, too, who had been present at Prestonpans, were ordered to attend, and to declare all they had observed. The examinations were taken in public in the great room at the Horse Guards, where any gentleman was permitted to enter, and where there were never less than one hundred and fifty auditors. The inquiry lasted five days, from ten in the morning till three in the afternoon. There were above forty witnesses examined. In the course of the proceedings public notice was often given, that if any person either knew or had been informed of any fact or circumstances contradictory to the evidence then given, it was a duty he owed to his king and country to acquaint the Board therewith. The Board at the same time declared that all such voluntary witnesses might feel assured of protection, and might at their option either give their information in public or in a private room by themselves.[1] I must add, too, that the Board ordered the whole of the correspondence between the Secretary of State for North Britain and Sir John Cope to be read and annexed to their report, lest letters omitted should contain such particulars as might explain de-

---

[1] Cope's Trial, Preface, p. viii.

tached passages in a different sense from what they bore when considered apart. Nay, further, when the inquiry was in all appearance finished, and the Board had adjourned to a distant day in order to give their opinion of the report, which was then in a good measure drawn up, one of them having accidentally heard that there was a person who asserted he had been present at the battle of Prestonpans, and who was said to relate many things differently from the witnesses examined by the Board, a summons was immediately sent him, and his examination taken and annexed to the report. . . . It was no small surprise to me to find on the inquiry that the various matters with which Sir John had been charged appeared so very different from my prepossessions about them. I could not impute this either to the partiality of the judges, the management of the accused, or the collusion of evidence. . . . However, as opinions once strongly imbibed are not easily departed from, I could not immediately persuade myself that a person whom I had long considered as extremely blamable was really so free from reproach as these examinations seemed to conclude; and therefore, still suspecting some fallacy, I did not rest satisfied till I had procured an authentic copy of all the evidence, such as it was, delivered by the Board to his Majesty."

The same gentleman who wrote the foregoing words elsewhere remarks regarding the majority of the witnesses: "They were all officers of the army that were in the action, the greatest part of them never accused or suspected of having any misconduct of their own to answer for, and yet great sufferers by the events of that day. It will, I suppose, be allowed that their losses, wounds, and imprisonments, and other disadvantages to which they were exposed by belonging to ruined regiments, were such inducements to have laid open the faults of their General as it was not in his power to have diverted or mitigated, especially as he was far removed from all influence over their fortunes or preferments." The writer might have added that the *esprit de corps* of the officers would have forced them to blame, if possible, the General, in order to save the credit of their regiments.

The Board, after hearing the statements of many civilians and officers—the Lord President Forbes being among the witnesses—declared that they were satisfied, and that the further evidence which was tendered by Sir John was unnecessary. Specifying in detail the charges which had been made against him, they found that he was not only guiltless on each point, but that his conduct was worthy of praise. One of the final sentences of their finding is, "That he did his duty as an officer, both before, at, and after the action : and that his personal conduct was without reproach." [1]

The same Board examined, separately and at length, into the cases of Fowke and Lascelles, the two surviving officers next in rank to the General, Gardiner having been slain. Their finding was that each of them had also discharged his duties with personal credit. On the three inquiries, as a whole, they concluded by reporting: "We are unanimously of opinion that Sir John Cope's behaviour has been unblamable; and that there is no ground for accusation against the said Sir John Cope, Colonel Peregrine Lascelles, or Brigadier-General Thomas Fowke." This verdict, which was commonly termed "the acquittal of Cope," was published at length in the 'London Gazette.' The writer of the description of the trial, from whom quotations have been made, did not, however, find that the publication of the mere finding of the Board effectually influenced the general belief in Cope's guilt; and—again to use his own expressions—as he had not spared to treat the character of Sir John Cope with great freedom whilst he believed him culpable, he thought it his duty, as an honest man, to make him the best reparation in his power, by publishing to the world the very same

[1] Cope's Trial, p. 102.

materials which had convinced himself of his error. He accordingly printed the evidence in full with a luminous preface, and appealed for its perusal to all who believed the wanton despoiling an innocent man of his character to be a crime. The king, too, showed that he still considered the General a trustworthy officer by appointing him to a high command in Ireland. But these efforts on the side of truth were of little avail in clearing his reputation. The Muses, as Burns remarked, were nearly all Jacobite. National prejudice was condensed into the following lines,[1]—

> "Say what reward shall be decreed
> For deeds like those of Sir John Cope.
> Reason and rhyme are all agreed—
> His ribband should be made a rope."

In the contemporary attacks on Sir John, however, there was often mixed with false history a vein of genuine humour, not always ill-natured. But modern writers of high standing have dealt with Cope's character in terms of unalloyed and unjust ferocity. For instance, Burton, in his 'History of Scotland,' after giving the current description of the battle of Prestonpans, makes the following remarks: "In the ordinary soldier, panic flight represents his own weakness, or

[1] Found in a contemporary manuscript, now in the British Museum (MS. of R. W. Ketton, Esq. of Fallbrig Hall).

the mismanagement of others. . . . Men will not cease to visit the general who flies, instead of abiding to keep order among his beaten troops or die if that be impossible, with infamy. . . . There arose deep alarm about the soundness of the British military system when it was learned that on this occasion several field-officers had fled from the Highland charge without looking behind them. Cope himself was excelled by others in the poltroonery with which his name is ever associated. He made some little efforts among the stragglers whom he found far away from the field to regulate a retreat, but others" (he selects the names of Brigadier-General Fowke and Colonel Lascelles) "seem to have fled right on."[1] And even more recently Professor Veitch, in glowing words, tells of Cope having been awakened from his sleep at Cockenzie by the news that the foe was attacking his army; of his riding in hot haste to the field; of Lochiel piercing impetuously the royalist line through a fire of cannon and musketry; of the advance of the famous Colonel Gardiner; of each Highlander receiving the thrust of his enemy's bayonet in the target where it stuck and cutting down his fronting foe; and finally, of Cope's boggling on horseback amid the lanes of Preston, and then, evidently permeated with the panic of the day,

[1] Vol. ii. p. 464.

flying and never halting until he put more than twenty miles behind him.[1] These fables are written by men in the full belief of their truth.

Sir John died in 1760, and was buried at the Church of St James's, Westminster, London. No monument marks his grave. The register simply records the burial on the 5th of August 1760 of "Sir John Cope, Knight of the Bath. M." — the last letter signifying "man." In the Chapel of Henry VII. at Westminster Abbey there is, nailed on the woodwork over a part of the wall, the small brass plate recording his installation as a Knight of that order. On it is emblazoned his coat of arms with the supporters then added to the armorial bearings of the family, which had been granted his ancestor, Sir William Cope, by the royal builder of the chapel, to whom he had been cofferer. From what is known historically of Sir John Cope's conduct, it may be confidently hoped that the brave, but much maligned, soldier was true to the motto appended to these arms —"Æquo adeste animo."

[1] Blackwood's Magazine, July 1894, p. 99.

ERRATA.

PAGE			
15	note	1.	*For* Dumfriesshire *read* Lanarkshire.
21	line	18.	*For* son *read* kinsman.
27	,,	2.	*For* William Grant of Prestongrange *read* Robert Dundas, younger of Arniston.
28	,,	8.	*For* 1745 *read* 1744.
46	,,	11.	*For* Sicilian *read* Sardinian.
67	,,	4.	*For* Glengarry *read* Lochgarry.
75	1st line of note.		*For* St Johnstoun *read* St John.
81	line	7.	*For* Sir Andrew *read* Sir Alexander.
84	last line of note.		*For* Buchan of Drumakill *read* Buchanan of Drumnakill.
95	*For last sentence of note substitute* He spent the night at Leckie House, and the following day marched to Falkirk.		
111	note.		*For* &c., p. 12, *read* p. 14, &c.
192	line	11.	*For* George *read* James.
229	,,	17.	*For* L[ord] R[egent, Prince Charles] *read* L[ord] N[airn].

Note.—In the references to Murray of Broughton's Narrative, the paging quoted is that of the proof-slips which were kindly lent to Sir Robert Cadell, and the following shows the pages as renumbered in the recently published volume :—

PAGE	NOTE	
108	1.	*For* p. 16 *read* p. 192.
170	1.	*For* pp. 17, 18 *read* p. 195.
187	1.	*For* p. 21 *read* p. 207.
198	1.	*For* p. 19 *read* p. 200.
204	1.	*For* p. 20 *read* p. 203.
225	1.	*For* p. 20 *read* p. 201.
245	1.	*For* p. 20 *read* p. 203.
257	1.	*For* p. 21 *read* p. 205.

www.ingramcontent.com/pod-product-compliance
Lightning Source LLC
Chambersburg PA
CBHW032055220426
43664CB00008B/1014